TRANSPORTATION INFRASTRUCTURE- ROADS, HIGHWAYS, BRIDGES, AIRPORTS AND MASS TRANSIT

COMMERCIAL AIRLINES: PASSENGER FEE ISSUES

TRANSPORTATION INFRASTRUCTURE-ROADS, HIGHWAYS, BRIDGES, AIRPORTS AND MASS TRANSIT

Additional books in this series can be found on Nova's website under the Series tab.

Additional E-books in this series can be found on Nova's website under the E-books tab.

TRANSPORTATION INFRASTRUCTURE- ROADS, HIGHWAYS, BRIDGES, AIRPORTS AND MASS TRANSIT

COMMERCIAL AIRLINES: PASSENGER FEE ISSUES

MICHAEL J. LIGUORI
EDITOR

NOVINKA

Nova Science Publishers, Inc.
New York

For permission to use material from this book please contact us:
Telephone 631-231-7269; Fax 631-231-8175
Web Site: http://www.novapublishers.com

Additional color graphics may be available in the e-book version of this book.

LIBRARY OF CONGRESS CATALOGING-IN-PUBLICATION DATA
Commercial airlines : passenger fee issues / editors, Michael J. Liguori.
p. cm.
Includes index.
ISBN 978-1-61761-989-2 (softcover)
1. Aeronautics, Commercial--United States--Finance. 2. Airlines--United States I. Liguori, Michael J.
HE9803.A5C66 2010
387.712--dc22
2010036420

Published by Nova Science Publishers, Inc. † New York

CONTENTS

PREFACE

Airlines have imposed a variety of fees on a range of optional services, such as checked and carry-on bags; meals; blankets; early boarding; and seat selection. According to airline officials, the fees are based on a combination of factors, including the cost of providing the service, competition, and consumer demand. The fees have supplemented airline revenues, providing at least $3 billion in 2009. However, information about the fees is not fully disclosed through all ticket distribution channels used by consumers, making it difficult for them to compare the total cost of flights offered by different carriers. This book addresses the nature and relationship to cost and disclosure of airline fees; the potential impact of such fees on the Airport and Airway Trust Fund; checked and mishandled baggage issues; and the process, if any, for refunding government-imposed taxes and fees when passengers do not use non-refundable tickets.

Chapter 1- To supplement fare revenues, airlines are increasingly charging fees for optional passenger services, notably for checked baggage, for which separate charges did not previously exist. While air fares are subject to a 7.5 percent excise tax that funds the Airport and Airway Trust Fund, which helps fund the Federal Aviation Administration (FAA), many new optional fees are not.

As requested, this report addresses (1) the nature, relationship to cost, and disclosure of airline fees, (2) the potential impact of such fees on the Airport and Airway Trust Fund, (3) checked and mishandled baggage issues; and (4) the process, if any, for refunding government-imposed taxes and fees when passengers do not use nonrefundable tickets. To perform this work, GAO analyzed financial data; reviewed applicable laws and regulations; and interviewed airline and government officials.

Chapter 2- The Subcommittee on Aviation will meet on Wednesday, July 14, at 2:00 p.m., in room 2167 of the Rayburn House Office Building to receive testimony regarding airline fees. The hearing will cover a number of issues pertaining to the trend of unbundling airfares to require passengers to pay for particular services individually. The hearing will also explore requirements for disclosure of fares, taxes, and fees, options for passengers to recover the costs of some fees, and revenue potentially available to the Airport and Airway Trust Fund (Trust Fund) if certain ancillary fees were subject to the Federal tax on airline tickets.

Chapter 3- Chairman Costello, Ranking Member Petri and Members of the Subcommittee: I am pleased to appear before the Subcommittee today to discuss the U.S. Department of Transportation's commitment to vigorous compliance and enforcement efforts to protect the rights of airline passengers. I will emphasize steps taken by the Department to ensure that airline passengers have accurate and complete information about the full cost of the air transportation they are purchasing, including the ancillary airlines fees they must pay.

First, let me emphasize the importance Secretary LaHood and this Administration place on the rights of airline consumers. From the start, we have carefully examined our regulatory authority to determine how best to assist airline consumers with the most serious problems they face, including lengthy tarmac delays, chronically delayed flights, and lack of consumer information on the on-time performance of flights. We decided to add clear limits on tarmac delays, tough rules on chronically delayed flights and more disclosure to passengers than had been proposed in the prior administration's rulemaking we inherited. In December 2009, we took the most forceful regulatory action then available to us by issuing a rule including those provisions

Chapter 4- Thank you for the opportunity to appear today before the Subcommittee in connection with its review of airline fees. Spirit is based in Fort Lauderdale, Florida. We currently have a fleet of 31 aircraft, serving 44 cities in the U.S., the Caribbean, Central and South America. We carry approximately 6.5 million passengers a year. Spirit believes that "unbundling" - *i.e.*, separating out optional customer services from the fare that are not essential to transporting a passenger allows customers the choice to purchase services or not - benefits the traveling public through lower total costs. This approach generates increased tax revenue by stimulating more travel. These unbundled services do not impose any costs on airport infrastructure, on the nation's air traffic control system or any other government services funded by the aviation federal excise tax. As such, no additional tax burden should be imposed on the cost of these ancillary services.

Chapter 5- Thank you for inviting Southwest Airlines to testify at today's hearing. My name is Dave Ridley. I'm Senior Vice President of Marketing and Revenue Management for Southwest Airlines and a Southwest Employee since 1988. In my role, I am accountable for the Company's topline revenue performance. My responsibilities include, among other things, pricing, advertising, and maintenance of our brand image as America's leading low fare, high Customer Service airline.

Southwest has been in the airline business for the past 39 years. We began operating in 1971 with three planes and one simple notion: If you deliver your Customers to their destinations when they want to get there, on-time, at a low fare – with friendly policies and even friendlier Employees – people will fly your airline.

Chapter 6- Mr. Chairman, Ranking Member Petri, and Members of the Subcommittee thank you for requesting that Business Travel Coalition (BTC) appear before you today to represent consumer and corporate managed travel interests on the subjects of airline product unbundling and extra fees for consumers.

My testimony today marks the 21st time BTC has been asked to provide testimony in Congress on competition, security and passenger rights issues. Today's hearing is by far the most important in terms of an issue's potential for harmful impacts to competition and consumers. BTC is not against unbundling as a matter of principle, but rather, it is opposed to the absence of disclosure of all fees and charges such that consumers cannot fully benefit from comparative shopping.

Chapter 7- Good afternoon, Mr. Chairman, Ranking Member Petri, and Members of the Subcommittee. The Interactive Travel Services Association (ITSA), American Society of Travel Agents (ASTA) and the Consumer Travel Alliance (CTA) all appreciate the opportunity to present our views on airline add-on fees and charges, and making them as transparent to consumers as possible.

My name is Kyle Moore, and I am the Vice President for Marketing of Sabre Holdings, owner of both the Sabre Network Global Distribution System (GDS), and Travelocity, an online travel company (OTC). Both are leaders in their fields, with our GDS, the largest in the United States, serving as the intermediary between airlines and other travel providers and thousands of travel agencies, including both traditional "brick-and-mortar" agencies and OTCs. All of those travel agency users rely on the computer reservations system provided by the Sabre GDS for timely, accurate and comprehensive air travel pricing and availability information on our nearly 400 participating airlines. Sabre is a long-time and active member of both ITSA and ASTA.

In: Commercial Airlines: Passenger Fee Issues ISBN: 978-1-61761-989-2
Editors: Michael J. Liguori

Chapter 1

COMMERCIAL AVIATION: CONSUMERS COULD BENEFIT FROM BETTER INFORMATION ABOUT AIRLINE-IMPOSED FEES AND REFUNDABILITY OF GOVERNMENT-IMPOSED TAXES AND FEES

United States Government Accountability Office

WHY GAO DID THIS STUDY

To supplement fare revenues, airlines are increasingly charging fees for optional passenger services, notably for checked baggage, for which separate charges did not previously exist. While air fares are subject to a 7.5 percent excise tax that funds the Airport and Airway Trust Fund, which helps fund the Federal Aviation Administration (FAA), many new optional fees are not.

As requested, this report addresses (1) the nature, relationship to cost, and disclosure of airline fees, (2) the potential impact of such fees on the Airport and Airway Trust Fund, (3) checked and mishandled baggage issues; and (4) the process, if any, for refunding government-imposed taxes and fees when passengers do not use nonrefundable tickets. To perform this work, GAO analyzed financial data; reviewed applicable laws and regulations; and interviewed airline and government officials.

WHAT GAO RECOMMENDS

If Congress wants to tax currently untaxed airline fees, it would need to amend the Internal Revenue Code. GAO recommends that DOT require airlines to consistently disclose optional fees and notify passengers of any refundable government fees; USDA determine whether its fee is refundable on unused nonrefundable tickets; and DHS issue guidance on the refundability of its fees. USDA and DHS agreed with the recommendations and DOT did not comment on them.

WHAT GAO FOUND

Airlines have imposed a variety of fees on a range of optional services, such as checked and carry-on bags; meals; blankets; early boarding; and seat selection. According to airline officials, the fees are based on a combination of factors, including the cost of providing the service, competition, and consumer demand. The fees have supplemented airline revenues, providing at least $3 billion in 2009—a small but growing amount of total revenues. However, information about the fees is not fully disclosed through all ticket distribution channels used by consumers, making it difficult for them to compare the total cost of flights offered by different carriers. The Department of Transportation (DOT) does not currently require disclosure of airline-imposed optional fees, apart from those for checked bags, but recently issued a Notice of Proposed Rulemaking (NPRM) considering different forms of disclosure of such fees. Meanwhile, a system is being tested to fully disclose all of the fees to consumers searching for fares, but airlines are not likely to disclose them unless compelled to do so.

Airlines' increasing reliance on fees reduces the proportion of their total revenue that is taxed to fund FAA. The Internal Revenue Service (IRS) has determined that many of these fees, including checked baggage fees, are not related to the "transportation of a person"—the basis for imposing the 7.5 percent excise tax. According to GAO's calculations, the checked baggage fee (the largest and only measurable untaxed fee) if taxed in fiscal year 2009 would have accounted for about 2 percent of total Trust Fund revenues but is likely to grow in future years given recent trends. Since DOT guidance requires airlines to report separately only revenues from baggage fees and reservation change and cancellation fees, GAO was unable to estimate potential collections from other untaxed fees.

Since airlines first imposed checked baggage fees, the number of checked bags per passenger has declined, contributing to a decline in the rate of mishandled bags. Despite the introduction of fees, airlines have not substantially changed their baggage service or compensation methods. Checked baggage fees have also led to greater amounts of carry-on baggage, resulting in greater competition for limited overhead storage space.

According to IRS, aviation excise taxes on unused nonrefundable tickets are not refundable, but if an airline refunds the ticket, a proportionate amount of tax may be refunded. In contrast, consumers with unused nonrefundable tickets with expired or lost value are entitled to a full refund of the September 11th Security Fee, but few consumers request a refund because airlines are not required to inform consumers of this. According to the Department of Homeland Security (DHS), applicable statutes and regulations authorize the refund of its customs and immigration inspection fees if services aren't rendered, but DHS has not issued any policy or guidance that makes this clear. The Department of Agriculture's (USDA) statutes and regulations are unclear as to whether its fee is refundable on unused nonrefundable tickets.

ABBREVIATIONS

ARC	Airlines Reporting Corporation
ATPCO	Airline Tariff Publishing Company
BTS	Bureau of Transportation Statistics
CBP	Customs and Border Protection
DHS	Department of Homeland Security
DOT	Department of Transportation
EMD	Electronic Miscellaneous Document
FAA	Federal Aviation Administration
GDS	Global Distribution System
IATA	International Air Transport Association
ICE	Immigration and Customs Enforcement
IRS	Internal Revenue Service
TSA	Transportation Security Administration
USDA	U.S. Department of Agriculture

July 14, 2010

The Honorable James L. Oberstar
Chairman
Committee on Transportation and Infrastructure
House of Representatives

The Honorable Jerry F. Costello
Chairman
Subcommittee on Aviation
Committee on Transportation and Infrastructure
House of Representatives

The Honorable Bill Pascrell, Jr.
House of Representatives

The U.S. passenger airline industry has been under tremendous financial pressure over the last decade, first from security threats that kept passengers away, then volatile fuel costs, and more recently falling demand due to an economic recession. In response, passenger airlines have adapted their business models. One significant change since 2008 is the introduction of fees for a variety of passenger services, such as a first or a second checked bag, for which separate charges did not previously exist. These fees represent an important source of revenues to U.S. passenger airlines, which collectively posted operating losses of $4.4 billion during calendar years 2008 and 2009.[1] During that same period, airlines reported approximately $7.9 billion in revenues from baggage fees and reservation change and cancellation fees—the two largest sources of fee revenues. However, the revenues from baggage fees, along with many other fees, are not subject to the 7.5 percent excise tax on amounts paid for domestic air transportation, the revenue from which is deposited in the Airport and Airway Trust Fund and which partially funds the Federal Aviation Administration (FAA), including the operation and development of the air traffic control system, among other things. In addition, the payment of separate fees by passengers, especially for checked bags, raises questions about whether the quality of checked baggage service has improved since baggage fees were introduced. The federal government also imposes various taxes and fees on passengers to help fund the costs of security, immigration, customs, and agricultural inspections, among other things.

However, the refundability of these fees is not always clear or communicated to airlines or consumers.

In this context, you asked us to address the following questions: (1) What is the nature and scope of the fees airlines charge to passengers, are the fees commensurate with the costs of the services provided, and are the fees transparent to passengers? (2) What is the potential impact of such fees on revenues available to the Airport and Airway Trust Fund? (3) What changes have taken place in the numbers of checked and mishandled bags, amount of compensation paid to passengers for mishandled bags, and other consumer issues since airlines began charging more widely for checked baggage? (4) What, if any, is the process for refunding government-imposed taxes and fees to passengers who do not use their nonrefundable tickets?

To address these objectives, we analyzed Department of Transportation (DOT) financial and operating data; reviewed applicable laws, regulations, and past studies; and interviewed officials from the airline industry, trade associations, consumer groups, global distribution system (GDS) companies, DOT, the Department of Homeland Security (DHS), U.S. Department of Agriculture (DHS), and the Internal Revenue Service (IRS). Specifically, to identify the nature and scope of airline-imposed fees, we developed a list of fees based on research of airline and travel Web Sites and corroborated the data in interviews with officials from 17 airlines.[2] To assess the potential impact of such fees on the Airport and Airway Trust Fund, we reviewed existing tax laws and regulations. We spoke with IRS officials about the applicability of the 7.5 percent excise tax imposed on amounts paid for the domestic air transportation of persons to the airline-imposed fees we identified. To examine issues with checked baggage, we reviewed data reported by airlines to the DOT's Bureau of Transportation Statistics (BTS), interviewed officials from BTS and other DOT offices, airlines and trade associations, and other interest groups about compensation for mishandled baggage. To identify mechanisms for returning government-imposed fees and taxes, we reviewed relevant agencies' applicable statutes, regulations, and guidance and interviewed officials from IRS, DHS's Customs and Border Protection (CBP), Immigration and Customs Enforcement (ICE), and Transportation Security Administration (TSA); and the U.S. Department of Agriculture (USDA) responsible for federal taxes and fees applied to airline tickets. We conducted this performance audit from October 2009 through July 2010 in accordance with generally accepted government auditing standards. Those standards require that we plan and perform the audit to obtain sufficient, appropriate evidence to provide a reasonable basis for our findings and conclusions based on our audit objectives. We believe that the evidence obtained provides a reasonable basis for our findings and conclusions based on our audit objectives. See appendix I for more information on our scope and methodology.

BACKGROUND

In recent years, airlines have faced challenging times as fuel costs increased followed by a steep decline in passenger demand due to the economic downturn. The U.S. passenger airline industry[3] incurred nearly $4.4 billion in operating losses during calendar years 2008 and 2009. Volatile jet fuel prices—the airlines' biggest operating expense in 2008—was the chief contributor to airline losses in 2008. Lower passenger traffic measured as enplanements, due to the economic downturn in 2008 and 2009, has also put pressure on many airlines' operating revenues and average 3rd quarter domestic airfares fell in 2009. See figure 1 for average 3rd quarter domestic airfares and domestic passenger traffic from 2000 through 2009.

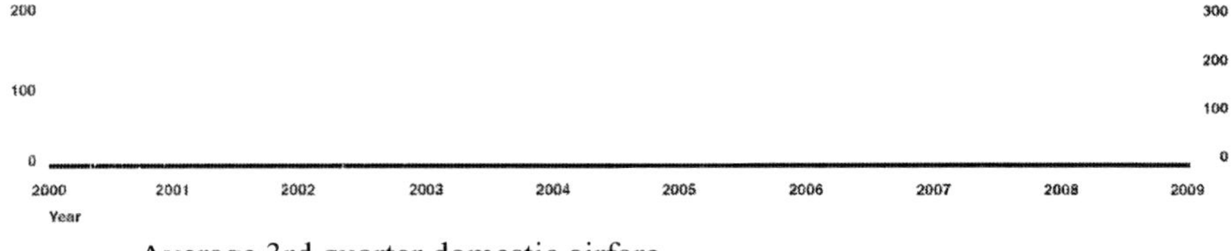

— — Average 3rd quarter domestic airfare
——— Millions of domestic passengers
Source: GAO analysis of DOT data.

Figure 1. U.S. Passenger Airlines Average 3rd Quarter Domestic Fares and Domestic Passengers, 2000-2009 (2010 dollars)

In response to these economic challenges, airlines began in 2008 to charge for many services for which separate charges did not previously exist.[4] These services include fees for a first or second checked bag, early boarding, seat selection and meals. Charges for other services, such as unaccompanied minors, reservation changes or cancellations, and oversized or overweight baggage, have existed in the airline industry for many years. In addition, other services that are assessed fees, such as for Wi-Fi access, are new offerings. Revenues from fees for all these services have supplemented airlines' fare revenues.

Airlines provide airfare information to the Airline Tariff Publishing Company (ATPCO), the tariff publishing house owned by a consortium of airlines, which, in turn, provides the fare information to GDSs[5] that package this information for use by online (for example, Expedia and Travelocity) and brick-and-mortar travel agencies and airline Web Sites. Once an airline ticket is purchased, the financial transaction is reconciled by the Airlines Reporting Corporation (ARC), another company owned by an airline consortium, which offers payment and settlement services for approximately 170 passenger airline and rail companies worldwide. However, while airfare information and some airline-specific information about fees for optional services is available on airline Web Sites and through GDSs, information on airlines' fees for the majority of optional services is available only through the airlines' Web Sites at booking and check-in, at their airport kiosks, and on board. Travel agencies, which sell the majority of airline tickets in the U.S., can provide fee information to customers only if the agents first search airline Web Sites or contact airline telephone reservation agents. Because airlines differ in how they impose fees for purchase of services, figure 2 depicts selected services and at what point they can currently be paid—during booking, at the airport, and onboard a flight. Fees for services can also be paid at other points besides those shown in the figure; for example, a passenger can often pay checked baggage fees when checking in online before departure.

DOT's Office of Aviation Enforcement and Proceedings (OAEP) enforces airline economic regulations, including advertising requirements related to the disclosure of the full fare to be paid by the consumer.[6] DOT requires government taxes imposed on an *ad valorem* (percentage) basis to be included in the advertised fare as well as those airline-imposed fees that are required to purchase a ticket, such as fuel surcharges and peak travel day charges.[7] In addition, in May 2008, DOT issued guidance which requires disclosure of fees and associated policies for checked baggage.[8] Additional DOT guidance also requires that U.S. passenger airlines report revenues from certain fees as part of their Form 41 quarterly financial filings to BTS. In accordance with this guidance, U.S. airlines are required to separately report revenues from baggage fees and reservation change and cancellation fees but not other optional service fees. DOT also prescribes regulations for U.S. airlines regarding the reporting of and compensation for passengers who have had mishandled baggage, for instance, baggage that is lost, damaged, or delayed. Major U.S. passenger airlines are required to report monthly to DOT the number of mishandled baggage reports filed with the carrier and DOT then publishes the data.[9]

DOT specifies that an airline cannot limit its liability for damages due to disappearance of, damage, or delay to lost baggage, to an amount less than $3,300 per passenger.[10] Compensation is subject to negotiation between the passenger and the responsible airline. TSA, which conducts security screening of checked bags, also submits monthly reports to DOT for mishandled baggage claims filed by passengers against TSA.[11] TSA reviews complaints to determine validity and compensation if TSA liability is determined.

Source: GAO.

Figure 2. Select Fees Imposed by U.S. Passenger Airlines and Example Locations Where Offered for Purchase

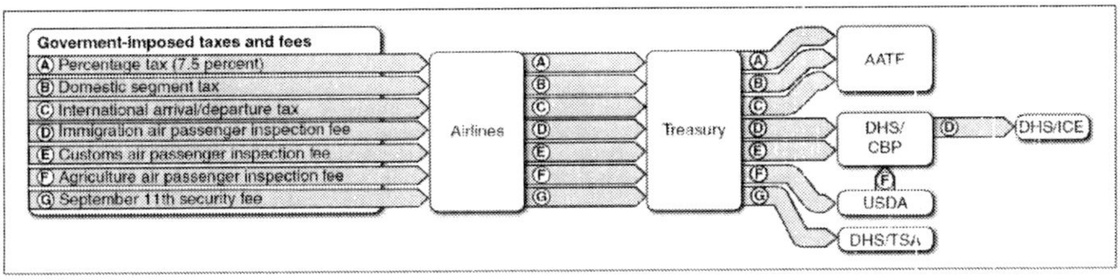

Source: GAO.

Figure 3. Distribution Path to Agency Accounts of Passenger-Paid Government-Imposed Taxes and Fees Collected by Airlines

The Internal Revenue Code imposes a 7.5 percent tax on amounts paid for the taxable transportation of a person for domestic air travel.[12] Treasury regulations and IRS guidance set general parameters for which airline fees are subject to the 7.5 percent excise tax. There is also a tax of $3.70 imposed on amounts paid for each segment of domestic travel,[13] and, if applicable, a tax on the use of international air travel facilities (also known as the international arrival/departure tax) of $16.10, for international travel that begins or ends in the United States.[14] Excise taxes collected by airlines are remitted to the IRS and deposited into the Airport and Airway Trust Fund, from which Congress funds FAA programs. FAA operates the air traffic control system, provides grants to airports, and oversees the safety of the industry. In addition to these excise taxes, the government imposes several fees on air travel that are collected by U.S. and foreign airlines and remitted to various other government departments and agencies. For example, TSA imposes the September 11th Security fee of $2.50 per enplanement, not to exceed $10 per roundtrip, for aviation security inspection services.[15] Other government-imposed fees are remitted to agencies including CBP and USDA to help pay for customs, immigration, and agricultural inspection activities respectively.[16] See figure 3 for the distribution to agency accounts of passenger-paid government-imposed taxes and fees collected by U.S. and foreign airlines.

New Fees for Optional Services Are Based on Cost and Other Factors and Are Not Always Fully Disclosed to Passengers at the Time of Booking

Airlines Have Introduced Fees for Services That They Previously Provided at No Charge as Well as for New Services

Increasingly, airlines are charging fees for a number of optional services for which separate fees did not previously exist. For example, before 2008, airlines' baggage fees generally extended only to passengers who checked a third bag or for overweight or oversized bags. However, since 2008, most airlines have implemented fees for both a first and a second checked bag. Currently, 15 of the 17 airlines we contacted charge $15 to $35 for the first checked bag and 16 of the 17 impose a fee of between $20 and $35 for a second checked bag. One airline recently stated that it will begin to charge up to $45 for a carry-on bag that does not fit underneath the seat. Collection of fees for reservation changes and cancellations, which range from $50 to $150, has grown since 2007. In addition, fees for services that were previously included in the fare paid have also been introduced. These services include meals costing between $2 and $10, telephone booking fees ranging from $5 to $25; and sleep sets, which go for $5 to $12, that include a pillow, blanket, sleeping mask, and earplugs. Appendix II includes information on a sample of optional service fees imposed by 17 airlines as of July 1, 2010.

Airlines are also charging for new services not previously available. For example, some airlines now offer in-flight wireless Internet access, onetime lounge access, and multiplying frequent flyer miles earned for a flight, for a fee. Some airlines are also selling service packages for annual subscription, for example, the option for passengers to pay an annual fee for checking up to two bags per flight as often as they fly with that airline within a year or for priority check-in and security screening. These services can also be purchased in combination and on a per-flight basis with fee amounts varying. For example, one airline offers priority boarding and security screening, free checked baggage allowance, extra seat legroom, and free alcoholic beverages for one fee. Airlines also provide a selection of fares that include specific optional services and benefits depending on the fare with higher fares including more services and benefits. Airlines are also offering third-party services such as hotel and car rental reservations and baggage pick-up and delivery, which can be purchased through the airline's Web Site.

Not all passengers are assessed service fees equally. For example, airlines waive some of these fees for elite members of their frequent flyer programs.[17] In addition, 13 of the 17 airlines we contacted do not charge these fees for their highest-paying passengers, such as those who hold first or business class tickets or full-fare economy class tickets. Airlines may also provide exemptions to select customers such as U.S. military personnel. Airline officials explained that customers who attain status with their airline's frequent-flyer program are likely to remain repeat customers if they are rewarded with service benefits such as baggage fee waivers.

Fees Have Proven Popular with Airlines as a Method of Generating Revenue While Maintaining Fare-Based Competition

According to financial data submitted by airlines to DOT, total revenue from baggage fees and reservation change and cancellation fees—the largest known sources of revenue for optional services—has increased since 2008 following widespread implementation of baggage fees in the United States. In calendar years 2008 and 2009, U.S. airlines collected nearly $3.9 billion in baggage fees and over $4 billion in reservation change and cancellation fees. Collection of fees for reservation changes and cancellations, although implemented prior to 2008, has risen sharply since then following the implementation of additional and/or higher fees for changing or canceling reservations. Accordingly, revenues from baggage fees and reservation change and cancellation fees have grown from less than 1 percent of operating revenues in 2007 to over 4 percent in 2009. Although small compared with total airline operating revenues, fee revenues are growing. In the first quarter of calendar year 2010, airlines reported $1.3 billion in baggage fees and reservation change and cancellation fees—a 13 percent increase from the corresponding quarter in 2009. Figure 4 shows the reported increase in revenues from baggage fees and reservation change and cancellation fees.

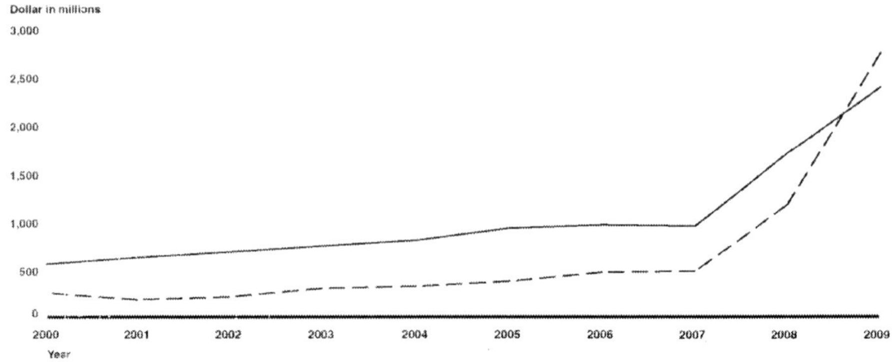

— — Reservation change and cancellation fee collections
——— Baggage fee collections
Source: GAO analysis of DOT Form 41 financial data.

Figure 4. Total Collections of Baggage Fees and Reservation Change and Cancellation Fees by U.S. Airlines, 2000-2009 (2010 dollars)

U.S. airlines must separately identify and report to DOT in their quarterly Form 41 filings only those revenues from baggage fees and from reservation change and cancellation fees, while other fee revenues are reported in a variety of other accounts that may also contain non-fee revenue. In 2009, BTS issued an accounting and reporting directive for U.S. passenger airlines to report ancillary revenues in a like manner. The directive allows airlines to report revenues from fees in different accounts such as in Transport-Related Revenues and Miscellaneous Operating Revenues that include revenue from other sources such as the sale of frequent flyer award miles.[18] Further, the guidance does not include all sources of ancillary revenues. Given this, we are unable to determine total revenues from other airline-imposed fees, such as those for telephone booking, seat selection, and early boarding. DOT has reported airline ancillary revenues were $7.8 billion in 2009, up from $5.5 billion in 2008. However, these reported revenues include not only those from the discrete accounts of baggage fees and reservation change and cancellation fees, but also fees from the Miscellaneous Operating Revenues account for such items as pet transportation and revenue from the sale of frequent flyer award program miles. Absent guidance that requires airlines to report revenues from fees in specific accounts, we found that there were differences among airlines in how some fee revenues were reported. For example, we found that telephone booking fees were reported as part of Reservation Cancellation Fees by some airlines and as Transport-Related Revenues by others. In addition, some airlines accounted for revenues from unaccompanied minors as Transport-Related Revenue, Transport Passenger Revenue or Miscellaneous Operating Revenue, while others reported it as part of Reservation Cancellation Fees, and one airline reported fees for unaccompanied minors as revenue from Excess Baggage Fees. Although there is a lack of clarity regarding the revenue amounts from most optional fees, not including those for baggage fees and reservation change and cancellation fees, it is likely that these revenues would be comparatively smaller because, according to airline representatives, these fee amounts are less than those for checked baggage or reservation changes and cancellations.

Airlines Have Imposed Fees, Which Are Partly Based on Costs, for Multiple Reasons

Several factors motivate airlines to make greater use of a pricing strategy that relies on charging fees for optional services. One factor airline officials told us is the opportunity to generate additional revenue while keeping fares lower. Airline officials said that by charging fees for services, they are able to keep fares lower than if fares were inclusive of checked baggage and other services as they had been in the past. Another factor airline officials told us is the ability to differentiate their customers' willingness to pay. In this way, customers that value the service can pay for it while customers that do not want to pay for the service don't purchase it. If airlines charged higher fares rather than charging for optional services, those passengers placing little value on optional services might decide not to purchase a ticket because there is more passenger resistance to higher fares, particularly during difficult economic times, than there is to paying for optional services. Airlines largely compete on their base ticket fares and passengers generally compare these fares when deciding which flight to purchase, often picking the lowest fare displayed. Several economic studies have found evidence that increases in the less transparent part of the price of a product—in this case optional service fees—has less of an effect on sales than increases in the price of the product itself—in this case, fares.[19] Officials from several airlines told us that another reason they impose fees is the ability to differentiate their airlines from their competition by providing some services for free and others at a fee.

Airlines that we interviewed indicated that costs were a consideration in setting fee levels, but other factors were also considered, such as competition and consumer demand. An official at one airline stated that the costs of providing services vary by airport and the routes served. For example, this official told us that the airline analyzes the costs of providing checked baggage service at each of the airports it serves and, while these costs differ, the airline sets a standard checked baggage fee to apply at all locations. Like prices for other products and services sold in a competitive market, fees for these services are also influenced by what competitors charge. Much like airfares, changes in fee amounts may be matched by competitors. In January 2010, Delta Air Lines increased its fee to check a first bag at the airport from $20 to $25, and within a month Continental Airlines, United Airlines, and American Airlines matched the increase. Furthermore, airlines evaluate consumer demand to determine what passengers are willing to pay for. One airline official told us that the airline conducts market research to determine whether a fee for a service would be acceptable to customers. This official said that the airline had eliminated a fee for the first checked bag on international flights and decreased the amount of a fee for its premium services based on customer feedback. Public discontent over a fee can also lead airlines to decide not to impose it. For example, Spirit Airlines announced that it will charge a fee for carry-on bags that cannot fit underneath a seat for travel beginning in August. In response to congressional and public outcry, 5 other airlines stated that they will not impose such a fee and to date no other airline has imposed a fee for carry-on bags.[20] Also, in 2008, US Airways tested consumer response by charging $2 for non-alcoholic beverages including sodas, juices, bottled water, and coffee, but discontinued after no other major airline began charging a fee for these drinks.

While airlines have collected a substantial amount of fee revenues, there is no clear link between the implementation of optional service fees and the profitability and financial stability of an airline. For example, American Airlines, Continental Airlines, Delta Air Lines, and Virgin America impose charges for checked baggage and other services, but each reported an operating loss for 2009. Not all profitable or financially stable airlines impose optional service fees. Southwest Airlines has not adopted a fee for a first or second checked bag, but continues to report an operating profit. On the other hand, both Spirit Airlines and Allegiant Air impose many fees for services on passengers and both also reported an operating profit for calendar year 2009.

Airlines recognize that their approach to offering services for a fee gives passengers choices that allow them to travel without paying the fees, such as by carrying bags into the cabin or by bringing their own meals onboard. Some passengers may prefer this approach in which they pay for only the services they want. One airline allows customers either to pay one higher price that includes the fare as well as services or to pay a lower fare for the flight and pay for services if desired. According to an official of this airline, 85 percent of that airline's customers prefer to pay the lower fare and pay for services separately.

Most Airline Fees for Services Are Not Incorporated in the Booking or Payment Process, Making It Difficult for Passengers to Compare Prices

Complete information on fees for optional services is not submitted by airlines filing their fare information with ATPCO or incorporated into the GDSs' fare offerings used by travel agencies. In contrast, all airline-imposed required charges, such as fuel surcharges and peak travel day charges, must be included in the advertised fare—the "full fare," or entire price to be paid by the consumer, regardless of distribution channel (airline or travel agent).[21] Unlike fare information, information on other service fees is not available through the GDSs with the exception of checked baggage, as discussed below, although it can be obtained from individual airlines by searching their Web Sites or contacting them directly. DOT does not specify in its advertising guidance that optional service fees be disclosed at ticketing with the exception of checked baggage fees and accompanying policies.[22] As a result, customers using online travel agencies and traditional or corporate travel agents, which together sell 60 percent of all airline tickets, cannot readily obtain and compare information on complete trip prices that include both the fare and selected service fees. This lack of information also makes it impossible for customers using online travel agencies or for travel agents using a GDS to select or make payment for optional services at the time of booking, which for many corporate customers is important for tracking payments. Travel agents and customers must then go directly to airline Web Sites to find out fee information.

Since checking a bag and the associated fees are deemed optional, they are not considered by DOT to be part of the "full fare" for purposes of its advertising rules, and therefore are not required to be disclosed prior to ticketing. However, DOT has required airlines and travel agents, including GDSs, to disclose checked baggage fees and accompanying policies at the time of purchase.[23] However, because this information is not filed with fare information by airlines, it is not readily available to GDSs and, therefore, to travel agents. DOT contends that travel agents utilizing a GDS can find this information by searching airline Web Sites, but GDS and travel agent officials we spoke with said that assuring that this information is accurate and up-to-date is time consuming and not practical if a customer is on the phone. Thus, even though travel agents are held to the same advertising and disclosure requirements as airlines, including those for checked baggage fees and policies, travel agents may not have information on checked baggage fees to accurately meet those requirements by relying on a GDS.

Recently proposed legislation would extend the disclosure requirements to include not only checked baggage fees, but also fees for seat assignments and other services that an airline may charge after the ticket is purchased.[24] In addition, legislation introduced in April 2010 would require the Secretary of Transportation to complete a rulemaking prohibiting airlines from charging fees for any carry-on baggage that falls within the restrictions imposed by the airline with respect to the weight, size, or number of bags, among other things.[25] Further, on June 8, 2010, DOT issued a Notice of Proposed Rulemaking (NPRM) that would, among a number of other things, if adopted, require U.S. and foreign airlines to disclose all fees for optional services, including those for checked baggage, advance seat assignments, and seat upgrades through a prominent link on their Web Site's homepage.[26] DOT also states in the proposed new rule that it is considering requiring that U.S. and foreign airlines make this fee information available to applicable GDSs.[27]

Travel Industry Efforts to Improve Fee Disclosure and Access Are Underway but May Not Lead to Full Disclosure

To improve travel agencies' ability to provide information on and payment for airline-imposed fees, ATPCO, the tariff publishing house, is working to include these fees as part of the information available in GDSs. ATPCO, which provides fare information to GDSs, has developed the Optional Services product—an automated approach to distribute fee information for flight-related services such as checked baggage and seat selection and for non-flight-related services such as lounge access. Airlines could then provide fee information to ATPCO, and, in turn, ATPCO could provide the information to the GDSs. When fully integrated into a GDS, travel agents, including corporate travel agents, could access and purchase optional services at the time of booking. Customers that purchase tickets at online travel agencies could also purchase optional services when booking tickets. This product would allow consumers to search airfares based on the total price of their trip rather than just the base airfare. Currently, 12 U.S. airlines constituting 79 percent of the operating revenues reported by U.S. airlines in 2009 are test filing this information with ATPCO, which is allowing GDSs to access it on a test basis.

In an attempt to ensure industry standards for the display, distribution, and financial settlement of fee transactions, ATPCO is coordinating its efforts with the International Air Transport Association (IATA)—a worldwide trade organization representing approximately 230 airlines—and ARC, which settles ticketing financial transactions. IATA has begun an initiative that would develop a standard for electronic transactions of miscellaneous documents, including those that contain airline-imposed fees. Stemming from its e-ticket effort, which eliminated the majority of paper-based ticketing transactions in June 2008, IATA is developing the Electronic Miscellaneous Document (EMD) standard, which will allow airlines and GDSs to electronically record fees that have been paid for optional services. Once this standard is incorporated by GDSs, customers using a corporate, online, or traditional travel agency would have the ability to pay for optional services at the time of ticketing. Use of the EMD will also facilitate miscellaneous financial transactions between airlines involving tickets that include transportation on more than one airline.

IATA anticipates that by the end of 2010, GDSs will be capable of issuing EMDs and by the end of 2012 all airlines will have EMD capability.

GDS companies have also developed their own products that accommodate fee information. For example, Sabre has developed a merchandising product that enables the consumer to comparison shop fares, including selections of optional services by incorporating ATPCO's Optional Services product. Consumers could select optional services as part of a fare search to compare airlines' offerings that include the fare and services. Sabre officials told us that its product is currently used in other countries, but no U.S. airlines have committed to providing fee information to ATPCO. Amadeus and Travelport—the next largest GDSs—have developed similar products that, according to officials with these companies, U.S. airlines have not committed to supporting.

GDS and travel agent representatives say that there is little incentive for airlines to disclose their fee information through the GDSs as such disclosure will increase the fare displayed to many passengers if fees are included. Airlines largely compete on fares and passengers compare fares when deciding which flight to purchase, often picking the lowest fare displayed. If one airline provided fee information and another did not, the airline that disclosed the fees would be at a disadvantage. Consequently, according to GDS representatives, it is unlikely that airlines will provide fee information or offer these services for sale through GDSs unless required to do so. In addition, trade associations are advocating that the airline industry work to standardize policies on fee disclosure and access. For example, the Interactive Travel Services Association, Business Travel Coalition and American Society of Travel Agents are leading efforts to have all fees available for sale through GDSs and to establish uniform codes for fee transactions. Similarly, the National Business Travel Association has supported efforts to make fees for services available through GDSs so that corporate travel agents can access and monitor fees when they are instituted or changed, buy services, and track them through their expense management systems.

Overall, we found that airlines we contacted were generally supportive of efforts to improve the transparency of fees for their customers. Officials from one airline indicated that providing the customer an opportunity to pay for additional services at the time of booking would create both greater choice and transparency while still allowing the airline to offer unbundled services. However, officials at another airline were more cautious indicating that the time of booking was not always the best point to sell additional services as passengers may not know at that time what additional services they will need. For example, they may not know how many, if any, bags they will check on the day of travel. Further, officials at another airline indicated that although they support transparency of optional service fees, the GDS environment may not be the best choice for distribution of this information, and there are alternatives to the GDS that can be cost effective to use to inform travel agents and passengers of fees for optional services. Officials from another airline stated that they are waiting until the testing of ATPCO Optional Services product has been completed before they decide whether to provide fee information to ATPCO. As noted earlier, DOT's June 2010 NPRM proposes greater fee disclosure and seeks comment on whether airlines should make this fee information available to applicable GDSs.[28] DOT officials told us that requiring fee disclosure provides additional information and resources to benefit consumers; however, imposing such a requirement must be weighed against the disadvantages of government interference with airline competition and the deregulated GDS environment.

Airlines' Increasing Reliance on Fees Reduces the Proportion of Total Revenue That Is Taxed to Fund FAA

Many Airline-Imposed Fees Are Not Subject to the 7.5 Percent Excise Tax

Unlike fares for domestic air transportation, a majority of the fee revenues collected by airlines on amounts paid by passengers for various airline services, including amounts paid for checked baggage, are not subject to the 7.5 percent excise tax,[29] in accordance with Treasury regulations and IRS guidance.[30] The Internal Revenue Code imposes a 7.5 percent excise tax on amounts paid for the taxable transportation of a person by air, the revenue from which is deposited into the Airport and Airway Trust Fund.[31] Treasury regulations, the last iteration of which were promulgated in the 1960s, set general parameters for which airline-imposed fees are subject to the 7.5 percent excise tax and which are not subject to the tax.[32] As a general rule, all amounts paid to the airline to procure domestic air transportation are part of the tax base unless exempted by regulation or IRS guidance. Generally, all mandatory charges necessary to transport passengers are included in the tax base,[33] but fees for optional services are not.[34] IRS has further clarified which airline-imposed fees are subject to the excise tax in guidance documents, including Revenue Rulings and Private Letter Rulings.[35] Treasury regulations and IRS guidance provide that revenue from many airline-imposed fees for airline services are generally not subject to the 7.5 percent excise tax, including fees for checked baggage, early boarding, phone reservations, and on-board meals.[36] On the other hand, amounts paid for other airline-imposed fees that are required as a condition of receiving domestic air transportation, such as some reservation change and cancellation fees, fuel surcharges, and peak travel day charges, are subject to the 7.5 percent excise tax in accordance with IRS guidance and applicable regulations,[37] and tax revenues from these fees are being deposited into the Trust Fund. See table 1 for a list of airline fees and surcharges on domestic air transportation that, pursuant to IRS guidance and Treasury regulations, are subject to the 7.5 percent excise tax.

Table 1. Airline-Imposed Fees and Surcharges on Domestic Air Transportation Subject to the 7.5 Percent Excise Tax According to IRS

Subject to 7.5 percent excise tax	Not subject to 7.5 percent excise tax
Fee to upgrade to higher class of accommodation (first or business class) An additional charge, paid in cash, for changing the class of accommodation is a payment for transportation and is subject to tax by regulation.[a]	**Fee for checked baggage** The fee is excluded from the tax base by regulation.[b]
Fee for ticket cancellation when passenger requests refund If an airline keeps a portion of the amount paid for a ticket as a cancellation fee when refunding the ticket amount to the customer, the consumer does not get a refund of tax already paid on that portion of the ticket amount (cancellation fee).[c] There is no additional tax on the amount retained.	**Fee for seat selection/seat preference within class of accommodation** If the service is optional and not a change in the class of accommodation, it is not included in the tax base.[d]
Fee for ticket change of destination or time of travel Additional charges for changing the destination or route, extending the time limit of a ticket, or as "extra fare" are payments for transportation and subject to tax by regulation.[e]	**Fee for early boarding within class of ticket purchased** As long as the fee for early boarding is optional, it is not included in the tax base.[f]
Fee for frequent flyer award redemption Service charge for a passenger to redeem frequent flyer miles.[g]	**Fee to apply already-purchased unused fare to new ticket** If a fee were charged so that the customer could apply the fare (on which tax was already paid) for an unused nonrefundable ticket to a new ticket, then that fee is not included in the tax base because it is optional.[h]

Table 1. (Continued)

Subject to 7.5 percent excise tax	Not subject to 7.5 percent excise tax
Fee for unaccompanied minors If the fee charged to provide support and care to an unaccompanied traveling minor is mandatory, such fee is taxable because the amount is paid as a condition of receiving air transportation. If it is optional, however, (e.g., for children of a certain age), then it is not included in the tax base.[i]	**Fee for reservation by phone; reservation by Internet** If the airline provides a mechanism for the customer to book travel for free, the use of a mechanism to book that charges a fee is then optional and the reservation fee is not subject to a tax. If there is no mechanism for the customer to book travel for free, the reservation fee is included in
Charge for peak travel/holiday travel The fee is subject to tax because it must be paid as a condition of receiving air transportation.[k]	**Fee for pet/animal transportation** The fee is treated as a baggage fee and not included in the tax base, per regulation.[l]
Fuel surcharge The charge is subject to tax because it must be paid as a condition of receiving air transportation.[m]	**Fee for standby** Assuming the fee is optional, the fee is not included in the tax base.[n]
	Fees for pillows and blankets The fees are not included in the tax base because they are for non- transportation service.[o]
	Charges for food and alcoholic beverages The charges are not included in the tax base because they are non- transportation services, as described in regulation.[p]

Source: GAO analysis of applicable statutes, regulations, and guidance.

Note: IRS determinations of the applicability of the 7.5 percent excise tax depend on the facts and circumstances of the imposition of the fee and, accordingly, may vary from airline to airline for similar services.

[a] 26 C.F.R. § 49.4261-7(c). See also Priv. Ltr. Rul. 118216-09.

[b] 26 C.F.R. § 49.4261-8(f)(1).

[c] Rev. Rul. 89-109; but see *United Airlines, Inc. v. U.S.*, 929 F. Supp. 1122 (N.D. Ill., 1996).

[d] Rev. Rul. 80-31.

[e] 26 C.F.R. § 49.4261-7(c).

[f] Rev. Rul. 80-31.

[g] Rev. Rul. 73-508. See also Priv. Ltr. Rul. 118216-09.

[h] Rev. Rul. 80-31. See also Priv. Ltr. Rul. 118216-09.

[i] Rev. Rul. 73-508. See also Priv. Ltr. Rul. 118216-09.

[j] Rev. Rul. 80-31. See also Priv. Ltr. Rul. 118216-09.

[k] Rev. Rul. 73-508.

[l] 26 C.F.R. § 49.4261-8(f)(1).

[m] Priv. Ltr. Rul. 118216-09 (Sept. 28, 2009); Rev. Rul. 73-508.

[n] Priv. Ltr. Rul. 118216-09; Rev. Rul. 80-31.

[o] 26 C.F.R. § 49.4261-8(f)(4).

[p] 26 C.F.R. § 49.4261-8(f)(4).

Potential Tax Revenues from Baggage Fees, If Taxed, Would Have Constituted Less Than 2 Percent of Total Trust Fund Revenues in Fiscal Year 2009

We estimate that if baggage fees, which generate the largest fee revenues reported to DOT, were subject to the 7.5 percent excise tax, the additional tax revenues collected in fiscal year 2009 would have contributed less than 2 percent of total Trust Fund revenues. In fiscal year 2009, airlines reported nearly $2.5 billion in fee revenue from checked baggage.[38] If baggage fees in that year had been subject to the 7.5 percent excise tax, an additional approximately $186 million[39] in excise taxes would have been credited to the Trust Fund. This amount is small—less than 2 percent—relative to the approximately $11 billion in revenue that the Trust Fund received during fiscal year 2009. However, this percentage is likely to grow because baggage fees have increased and some airlines have introduced additional service fees. For example, in the first quarter of calendar year 2010, airlines reported a 33 percent increase in revenues from baggage fees compared to the same quarter in 2009.

As noted earlier, aside from checked baggage, DOT guidance does not require airlines to separately report revenues received from fees for services that have not to date been considered part of the transportation of persons—such as early boarding, seat selection, and standby—and these revenues are also not subject to the 7.5 percent excise tax according to IRS. Thus, we cannot be certain how much additional revenue Treasury might have collected and credited to the Trust Fund if that tax had been applicable to all these fees.

Extending Scope of the 7.5 Percent Excise Tax Would Require Legislative or Regulatory Changes

The Internal Revenue Code defines taxable transportation in terms of the arrival/departure of the transportation, but does not define or discuss what is "amount paid for taxable transportation of any person."[40] Treasury regulations provide examples of what payments are and are not subject to the 7.5 percent excise tax.[41] Treasury regulations regarding the scope of payments for transportation subject to the 7.5 percent excise tax were established in the 1960s at a time of a regulated and very different airline industry. In light of changes in airline pricing, the Treasury regulations do not discuss many of the fees currently charged by airlines. The recent IRS private letter ruling, which provides some clarification of the applicability of the excise taxes to examples of current airline fees, is based on the facts and circumstances presented to IRS by the letter ruling requester and is not fully applicable to all fees airlines may charge. Without a statutory change with explicit directions on what fees are to be subject to the 7.5 percent excise tax, each new airline fee, or even the facts and circumstances of how each airline charges current fees, may require interpretation on a case-by-case basis as to whether or not to impose a tax. Therefore, eventual effects on the Trust Fund remain unknown.

IMPOSITION OF CHECKED BAGGAGE FEES HAS CONTRIBUTED TO DECREASE IN THE RATE OF MISHANDLED BAGS AND MORE CARRY-ON BAGS

Since Checked Baggage Fees Were Implemented, the Reported Rate of Mishandled Baggage Has Declined

The introduction of checked baggage fees has, by several estimates, led to fewer checked bags, which, among other factors, has contributed to a decline in the number of mishandled bags per 1,000 passengers.[42] Some airline officials told us that the number of checked bags per passenger has decreased since the checked baggage fees were implemented. One airline official said checked baggage had decreased by half and officials at another airline reported the number of checked bags per passenger had decreased by 40 percent. As a result, the rate of mishandled bags per 1,000 passengers has declined since baggage fees were widely implemented. According to data submitted by airlines to DOT, the reported rate of mishandled bags per 1,000 passengers varied from 2000 through 2007 and declined 40 percent (from 7 per 1,000 to less than 4 per 1,000) from 2007 through 2009.[43] Figure 5 shows the decrease in the reported rate of mishandled bags per 1,000 passengers from 2000 through 2009 for U.S. airlines reporting to DOT.

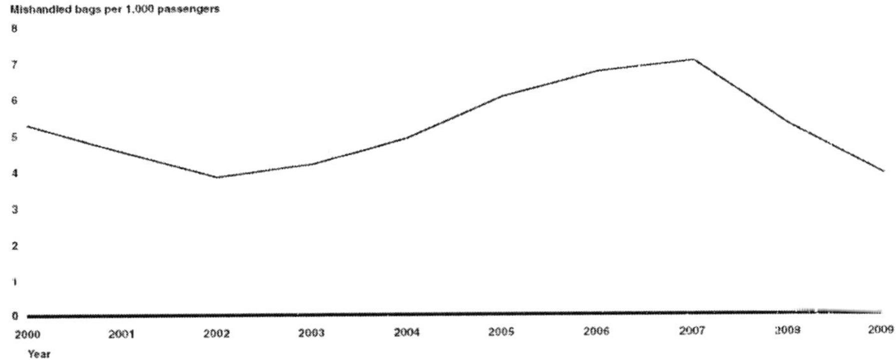

Source: GAO analysis of DOT data.

Figure 5. Reported Rate of Mishandled Bags per 1,000 Passengers for Reporting U.S. Airlines, 2000-2009

Airline Policies Differ in How Compensation to Passengers for Mishandled Bags Is Determined and Have Not Changed Due to the Introduction of Baggage Fees; TSA also Reviews Mishandled Bag Claims

Airline policies to compensate passengers in case of mishandled baggage, as outlined in their contracts of carriage, differ in the assistance to passengers and in the process for determining compensation.[44] For instance, 7 of the 17 airline contracts of carriage that we reviewed specify that baggage will be delivered if delayed, whereas the remaining 10 are silent on the issue.[45] In addition, 10 airline contracts state that efforts will be made to return delayed baggage within 24 hours, whereas the remaining 7 contracts do not specify a time frame. Airline policies on how passengers are compensated for mishandled bags are all subject to DOT's regulatory requirement that precludes airlines from limiting their liability for damages due to disappearance of, damage, or delay to checked baggage, to less than $3,300 per passenger.[46] However, other than this requirement, DOT does not currently specify baggage policies to include in contracts of carriage. DOT conducts random on-site investigations at airlines for compliance with domestic and international air travel rules and has completed 15 investigations in the past 2 years with 7 planned investigations for fiscal year 2010. DOT investigations result in either an enforcement order assessing civil penalties and specifying what the airline must do to be in compliance if problems are found or a notice letter to the airline when minor or no problems are found. DOT has no detailed requirements for how compensation should be determined, instead allowing baggage liability issues between passengers and airlines to be resolved through negotiations and in the courts.[47] Furthermore, most airline officials reported that they have not adjusted their compensation policies for mishandled baggage since baggage fees were implemented because, according to some officials, the service provided has not changed. When asked whether DOT should specify airline compensation policies in cases of mishandled baggage in contracts of carriage, the agency responded that it has the authority to act against particular practices on a case-by-case basis and has done so with individual enforcement actions and industry letters to airlines. For example, in October 2009 DOT sent an industry letter to airlines advising that it had become aware of certain policies, such as denied reimbursement for necessities when the baggage is expected to reach the passenger within 24 hours, limited reimbursement to actual expenses up to a fixed maximum amount per day after the first day, and passenger reimbursement for incidental expenses only on the outbound leg of a roundtrip flight—all of which are considered arbitrary limits on expense reimbursement in violation of DOT guidance.[48] DOT's recent proposed rulemaking seeks comment on requiring carriers to include minimum standards in their customer service plans that would reimburse passengers for baggage fees if the baggage is lost or not timely delivered as well as establishing a definition for when a bag is not "timely delivered."[49]

Checked Baggage Fees Have Led to an Increase in Carry-on Baggage and Flight Crew Concerns Regarding Crew and Passenger Safety

According to some airline officials, since checked baggage fees were imposed, there has been an increase in carry-on baggage because some passengers who have chosen not to check a bag for a fee have instead brought bags into the cabin. Airline policies generally state that a passenger can carry on board one bag and one personal item.[50] An employee union representing flight attendants noted that this increase in carry-on baggage can slow passenger boarding and adversely affect the safety of passengers and flight attendants. In a recent survey by the Association of Flight Attendants, more than half of the responding flight attendants cited excess and oversized or overweight carry-on bags. The survey respondents also reported concerns with full overhead bins, an increase in checked bags at the gate, pushback delays, and stressful boarding situations. Almost one-third of the responding flight attendants reported concerns about injuries to airline staff and passengers from lifting carry-on bags.[51] As noted earlier, Spirit Airlines has introduced a fee for carry-on baggage—a policy that the carrier asserts is at least in part aimed at reducing the amount of carry-on baggage.

Refundability of Government-Imposed Taxes and Fees is Not Always Clear and Communication of Refund Eligibility to the Airlines and Consumers is Lacking

The refundability of government-imposed taxes and fees on unused nonrefundable tickets varies depending on the tax or fee. TSA's September 11th Security Fee, which funds passenger aviation security services, is the only government-imposed fee or tax that is clearly refundable on unused nonrefundable tickets that expire or lose their value, according to TSA.[52] However, according to airline officials, the security fee is rarely refunded because its refundability is not well known by consumers, and a refund is only provided if a passenger requests a refund from the airline.[53] The IRS states that the aviation excise taxes—the 7.5 percent ticket tax, passenger segment tax, and international arrival/departure tax that fund FAA activities—are not refundable on unused nonrefundable tickets; however, to the extent that a portion of the ticketed fare is refunded, the collected tax attributable to that portion of the fare may be refunded to the passenger.[54] Thus, if airline policy allows a passenger to apply part of the fare for an unused nonrefundable ticket as a credit for future travel on the airline, the passenger receives a credit for the proportionate share of the taxes applied to the next ticket (less a change fee) and thus does not have to pay the taxes a second time. If, however, a passenger does not use the credit, the passenger may not receive a refund of the taxes. For example, according to DOT, some airlines offer a credit for the price of the ticket, including taxes and fees, minus a reservation change or cancellation fee and the difference in fares. Normally, passengers have to notify the airline prior to flight departure to qualify for a credit which is valid for 1 year for travel on the airline. However, these airlines would not provide a refund in cash of the ticket price. Because the excise tax is imposed on amounts paid for air transportation and not connected to the transportation itself, taxes paid on unused purchased tickets remain in the Airport and Airway Trust Fund.

In regards to other government-imposed fees, according to CBP, which administers the Customs Air Passenger Inspection Fee and the Immigration Air Passenger Inspection Fee, applicable statutes and regulations authorize the refund of these fees on unused nonrefundable tickets. In the past, as CBP officials noted, the agency has allowed for such refunds and CBP indicated that they would not consider the refund of its fees to be improper insofar as fees can be refunded if inspection services are not provided. However, CBP has not issued policy or guidance that clarifies this practice or whether airlines can or must refund fees if requested by consumers. Additionally, CBP told us that when airlines do refund fees to passengers, it accounts for those with CBP as a "credit" on a subsequent submission of collected fees. In contrast, with respect to the Animal and Plant Health Inspection User Fee, USDA officials said that airlines may have refunded consumers this fee on occasion but do not know the circumstances of this and acknowledge that their controlling statute is silent on this issue. In regards to all of these fees, airline officials told us that they have received few, if any, requests for fee refunds. An official of a trade association that represents travel agencies told us that there is confusion about whether government-imposed taxes and fees are refundable. As a result, this official said, many travel agents state that they do not try to recoup taxes and fees on unused nonrefundable tickets for their customers. Table 2 shows government-imposed taxes and fees, their amounts, and agencies' interpretations of their refundability.

Airlines Are Not Required to Notify Consumers That They May Be Eligible for Refunds

Although applicable TSA guidance requires the refund of the September 11th Security Fee on unused nonrefundable tickets that expire or lose their value, at the passenger's request, consumers are generally unaware that they may be eligible for a refund. According to TSA, regulations require airlines to refund the fee to consumers when a change in their itinerary occurs, but this occurs automatically.[55] We asked airline officials to describe the process by which they refund TSA fees to consumers and asked if consumers have requested refunds. Some airlines replied that they have not been requested by consumers to refund the fee and others were not aware that consumers were entitled to a refund but if requested they would issue one. We asked TSA officials why no policy has been developed to notify consumers of their rights. TSA responded that current refund policy sufficiently ensures that refunds will be provided upon request by the airline and TSA has not received complaints regarding an airline failing to comply with TSA regulation and guidance regarding refunds. Similarly, while CBP allows airlines to refund the customs and immigration inspection fees on unused nonrefundable tickets, because the agency has not communicated this to airlines or the public, consumers are unaware that they fees can be requested. We believe that given that consumers are not notified of a potential refund, they may be unlikely to realize their entitlement to such and, thus, would be unlikely to request a refund. DOT has the authority under 49 U.S.C. § 41712 to prohibit unfair or deceptive practices or unfair methods of competition and DOT believes ensuring that consumers are not mislead regarding their rights to refunds is within the scope of this authority. However, DOT staff point out that it has received few, if any, complaints about refundable government fees.

CONCLUSIONS

Airlines are increasingly charging fees for optional services that were previously provided without a separate charge. These fees, which may be paid at the time of booking, at check-in, or onboard, are not uniformly disclosed to passengers through the various distribution systems available to purchase tickets. DOT's current guidance does not require disclosure of airline-imposed optional service fees apart from those for checked bags although the agency issued a Notice of Proposed Rulemaking in June 2010 requesting public comment on this issue. Because information on some of these fees for optional services may be available only through airline Web Sites and not through the global distribution systems used by passengers who purchase tickets through online travel agencies or by travel agents, passengers may have difficulty calculating the total price of a trip and comparing prices among airlines. Making complete, clear, and uniform information on airline fees available through travel agents and airline Web Sites would enable passengers to make fully informed choices about travel options.

Table 2. Government-Imposed Taxes and Fees and Amounts Paid by Passengers and Legal Basis for Their Refundability on Unused Nonrefundable Tickets

Government-imposed tax/fee	Refund of government-imposed tax/fee authorized?
Passenger Ticket Tax[a] The law imposes a tax of 7.5 percent on the ticketed fare for flights within the continental U.S. or Canada/Mexico 225-mile buffer zone, with certain exceptions;[b] this amount is deposited in the Airport and Airway Trust Fund that primarily funds FAA activities.	No.[c]
Passenger Segment Tax[d] The law imposes a tax of $3.70 per domestic flight segment; this amount is deposited in the Airport and Airway Trust Fund that primarily funds FAA activities.	No.[e]
International Arrival/Departure Tax[f] The law imposes a tax of $16.10 per passenger for all flights arriving in or departing from the United States, Puerto Rico, or the U.S. Virgin Islands; this amount is deposited in the Airport and Airway Trust Fund that primarily funds FAA activities.	No.[g]
September 11th Security Fee[h] TSA imposes $2.50 per enplanement not to exceed $5 one-way or $10 roundtrip for aviation security inspection services.[i]	Yes.[j]
Customs Air Passenger Inspection Fee[k] A $5.50 fee is imposed for the arrival of each passenger aboard a commercial aircraft from a place outside the United States, with certain exceptions, for customs inspection services.	Yes. According to CBP, relevant statutes authorize airlines to refund fees if services are not rendered and have allowed for refunds in the past. However, CBP has not issued policy or guidance that clarifies this practice

Table 2. (Continued)

Government-imposed tax/fee	Refund of government-imposed tax/fee authorized?
	or whether airlines can or must refund fees if requested by consumers.
Immigration Air Passenger Inspection Fee[l] A $7 fee is assessed for each passenger arriving at a port of entry in the United States, or for the pre-inspection of a passenger in a place outside of the United States prior to such arrival for immigration inspection services.	Yes. According to CBP, relevant statutes authorize airlines to refund fees if services are not rendered and have allowed for refunds in the past. However, CBP has not issued policy or guidance that clarifies this practice or whether airlines can or must refund fees if requested by consumers.
Animal and Plant Heath Inspection User Fee[m] USDA imposes $5 per passenger upon arrival from a place outside of the customs territory of the United States for its health inspection services.	Unclear. According to USDA, relevant statutes and regulations are silent as to whether the fee is refundable on unused nonrefundable tickets.

Source: GAO analysis.

[a] 26 U.S.C. §§ 4261(a), 4262(a).

[b] 26 U.S.C. §§ 4261(a), 4262.

[c] Rev. Rul. 89-109.

[d] 26 U.S.C. § 4261(b). A domestic flight segment consists of one take-off and one landing.

[e] Officials with IRS stated that the reasoning of Rev. Rul. 89-109 is applicable here.

[f] 26 U.S.C. § 4261(c). Section 4261(c)(3) provides a modified international arrival/departure tax rate of $8.10 for domestic flights beginning or ending in Alaska or Hawaii.

[g] Officials with IRS stated that the reasoning of Rev. Rul. 89-109 is applicable here.

[h] 49 U.S.C. § 44940, 49 C.F.R. part 1510.

[i] 49 C.F.R. § 1510.5.

[j] See Letter from Randall Fiertz, Transportation Security Administration, Acting Director of Revenue, to James Hultquist, Air Transport Association, Managing Director, Taxes, November 21, 2002, Docket No. TSA-02-11120-59. TSA is considering promulgating further details on refunds under the Final Rule for 49 C.F.R. part 1510, which has yet to be issued.

[k] 19 U.S.C. § 58c(a)(5)(A), 19 C.F.R. § 24.22(g).

[l] 8 U.S.C. § 1356(d), 8 C.F.R. § 286.2(a).

[m] 21 U.S.C. § 136a, 7 C.F.R. § 354.3(f).

While certain airline fares are subject to the 7.5 percent excise tax, this tax does not apply to many airline-imposed fees, and consequently the Airport and Airway Trust Fund receives less revenue than if that tax applied to all fee revenues. IRS has determined that fees for checked baggage and many other services not currently considered to be part of the transportation of a person are not subject to the 7.5 percent excise tax. If baggage fees alone had been subject to the 7.5 percent excise tax in fiscal year 2009, the Trust Fund would have received approximately an additional $186 million in revenues. This amount is expected to grow in future years if airlines continue to shift toward more fee revenue relative to fare revenue.

It is hard to determine the amount of total fee revenues that airlines collect. Currently revenues from fees other than baggage fees and reservation change and cancellation fees are reported in miscellaneous and other accounts that also include revenues from non-fee sources. The BTS accounting and reporting directive on ancillary fees allows airlines to report in their quarterly financial filings to DOT revenues from most fees in various accounts. Not having a clear accounting makes it difficult for policymakers and regulators to determine total revenues from airline-imposed fees and the impact on the airline industry.

Finally, TSA's security fee is refundable on unused, nonrefundable tickets that expire or lose their value; however, there is currently no requirement or process in place to alert passengers that they are eligible for such refunds. Additionally, relevant statutes and regulations authorize CBP, via the airlines, to refund its customs and immigration fees but has not issued any policy or guidance that clarifies this. Finally, it is unclear if USDA's agricultural inspection fee is refundable. Without this guidance and determination of the refund eligibility of USDA's fee, consumers are not aware the fee is refundable and consequently may not be receiving refunds to which they may be entitled.

MATTER FOR CONGRESSIONAL CONSIDERATION

If Congress determines that the benefit of added revenue to the Airport and Airway Trust Fund from taxation of optional airline service fees, such as baggage fees, is of importance, then it should consider amending the Internal Revenue Code to make mandatory the taxation of certain or all airline imposed fees and to require that the revenue be deposited in the Airport and Airway Trust Fund.

RECOMMENDATIONS FOR EXECUTIVE ACTION

We are making six recommendations to the Departments of Transportation, Homeland Security and Agriculture.

To improve the transparency of information on airline-imposed fees and government-imposed taxes and fees for consumers and improve airlines' reporting of fee revenues to the Department of Transportation, we recommend the Secretary of Transportation take the following four actions:

- Improve the disclosure of baggage fees and policies to passengers, in accordance with DOT guidance, by requiring that U.S. airlines and foreign airlines that fly within or to or from the United States disclose baggage fees and policies along with fare information such that this information can be consistently disclosed across all distribution channels used by the airline.
- Require U.S. airlines and foreign airlines that fly within or to or from the United States to disclose all airline-imposed optional fees that it deems important to passengers to know and further require that this information be consistently disclosed across all distribution channels used by the airline.
- Require that U.S. passenger airlines and foreign airlines that fly within or to or from the United States consistently disclose to passengers, applicable government-imposed fees on unused nonrefundable tickets that may be eligible for refunds once these determinations are made by relevant agencies.
- Require U.S. passenger airlines to report to DOT all optional fees paid by passengers related to their trip in a separate account, exclusive of baggage fees and reservation change and cancellation fees.

To eliminate the ambiguity regarding the refund of government-imposed fees to purchasers of unused nonrefundable tickets, we recommend that the Secretary of Homeland Security issue guidance regarding the refundability of the customs and immigration inspection fees to U.S. and foreign airlines collecting these fees.

To eliminate the ambiguity regarding government-imposed fees that are eligible for refund to purchasers of unused nonrefundable tickets, we recommend that the Secretary of Agriculture determine whether a passenger is eligible for a refund of the animal and plant heath inspection fee and convey this determination to U.S. and foreign airlines collecting these fees.

APPENDIX I: SCOPE AND METHODOLOGY

We were asked to answer the following research questions: (1) What are the nature and scope of the fees airlines charge to passengers, are the fees commensurate with the costs of the services provided, and are the fees transparent to passengers? (2) What is the potential impact of such fees on revenues available to the Airport and Airway Trust Fund? (3) What changes have taken place in the numbers of checked and mishandled bags, amount of compensation paid to passengers for mishandled bags, and other consumer issues since airlines began charging more widely for checked baggage? and (4) What, if any, is the process for refunding government-imposed taxes and fees to passengers who do not use their nonrefundable tickets? To address these objectives, we analyzed airline financial and operating data; reviewed applicable laws, regulations, and past studies; and interviewed officials from the airline industry, the Department of Transportation (DOT), the Internal Revenue Service (IRS), the Department of Homeland Security (DHS), and the U.S. Department of Agriculture (USDA). Our financial analysis relied on airline financial information reported to DOT by airlines from calendar year 2000 through calendar year 2009—the most recently available. We used the Department of Commerce's chain-weighted price index for gross domestic product to adjust dollar figures to 2010 dollars to account for changes over time in the price level of the economy. To assess the reliability of the DOT Bureau of Transportation Statistics (BTS) data, we reviewed the quality control procedures applied by BTS and determined that the data were sufficiently reliable for our purposes.

To identify the nature and scope of airline-imposed fees, we developed a list of fees based on research of travel and 17 airline Web Sites and corroborated the data in interviews with officials from airlines.[56] In interviewing the airline officials, we used a semi-structured interview instrument, which asked questions pertaining to airline-imposed fees and how fee amounts were set. We correlated and assembled the results of the interviews so that airline proprietary information was not disclosed. To assess what is required in the disclosure of airline-imposed fees, we analyzed applicable laws and regulations and interviewed officials from DOT's Office of Aviation Enforcement and Proceedings, which establishes laws and guidance related to full disclosure advertisement rules. To assess travel industry efforts to improve fee disclosure and policies, we interviewed officials from the Air Transport Association, International Air Transport Association, Airline Reporting Corporation, Airline Tariff Publishing Company, Sabre, Travelport, Amadeus, Interactive Travel Services Association, Business Travel Coalition, American Society of Travel Agents, and FlyersRights Organization.

To assess the potential impact of such fees on the Airport and Airway Trust Fund, we reviewed existing tax laws and regulations and spoke with IRS officials about the applicability of the excise taxes imposed on amounts paid for air transportation of persons to the airline-imposed fees we identified. We then calculated the potential impact in the most recent complete fiscal year (2009), on the Airport and Airway Trust Fund if revenues from baggage fees—revenues that airlines are required by DOT to report separately and that are not currently taxed—had been taxed at the 7.5 percent excise tax applied to fare revenues. We did not calculate the impact on the Trust Fund of taxing revenues from reservation change and cancellation fees, which are also reported separately, because these revenues are currently subject to the 7.5 percent excise tax. In addition, we were unable to calculate the impact on the Trust Fund if revenues from other currently untaxed fees had been taxed as these fee revenues are not required by DOT to be reported separately and some airlines in our sample did not provide this information to us when we requested it. We also spoke with IRS officials regarding what actions could be taken that would make currently untaxed fees subject to the 7.5 percent excise tax.

To examine issues with checked baggage, we reviewed data reported by airlines to DOT, and subsequently published in DOT's Air Travel Consumer Report. To assess the reliability of this data we interviewed DOT personnel regarding quality control procedures, and subsequently determined that the data were reliable for our purposes. We also interviewed DOT officials from BTS and the Office of Aviation Enforcement and Proceedings, DHS's Transportation Security Administration (TSA), airlines, trade associations, and other interest groups about compensation for mishandled baggage. We reviewed regulations and policies regarding checked baggage liability and disclosure requirements. We also conducted a content analysis of the results of an open-ended question on a survey conducted by the Association of Flight Attendants in February 2010 on the impacts of carry-on baggage. Our analysis enumerated the percentage of the 800 respondents that reported on excessive carry-on baggage and its implications on boarding processes and in-cabin injuries. We reviewed the methodology and data collection instrument used by the Association of Flight Attendants in gathering this information, and determined that the data collected from the 800 open-ended responses was sufficiently reliable for our use. We also conducted an analysis of the contract of carriage of the 17 airlines in our sample. These contracts of carriage were accessed on each airline Web Site and information was corroborated in our interviews with airline officials.

To identify mechanisms for refunding government-imposed fees and taxes, we reviewed relevant agencies' statutes and guidance and interviewed officials from IRS, DHS Customs and Border Protection, Immigration and Customs Enforcement, TSA, and the USDA who are responsible for federal taxes and fees applied to airline tickets. We also interviewed airlines and trade associations on the process for refunding eligible government-imposed taxes and fees. We conducted this performance audit from October 2009 through July 2010 in accordance with Generally Accepted Government Auditing Standards. Those standards require that we plan and perform the audit to obtain sufficient, appropriate evidence to provide a reasonable basis for our findings and conclusions based on our audit objectives. We believe that the evidence obtained provides a reasonable basis for our findings and conclusions based on our audit objectives.

APPENDIX II: SAMPLE OF AIRLINE-IMPOSED FEES FOR OPTIONAL SERVICES

Table 3. Domestic Checked Baggage Fees of 17 U.S. Airlines as of July 1, 2010

Airline	First bag (airport/online)	Second bag (airport/online)	Additional bags (each)	Overweight bags	Oversized bags
Air Tran	$15	$25	3+: $50	51-70 lbs: $49 71-100 lbs: $79	$49-$79
Alaska[a]	$20	$20	3: $20 4+: $50	51-100 lbs: $50	$50-$75
Allegiant	$35/$15-$30	$35/$25-$35	$35/$50	51-74 lbs: $50 75+ lbs: $100	$35
American	$25	$35	3-5: $100 6+: $200	51-70 lbs: $50 71-100 lbs: $100	$150
Continental	$25/$23	$35/$32	3+: $100	51-70 lbs: $50	$100
Delta	$25/$23	$35/$32	3: $125 4-10 $200	51-70 lbs: $90 71-100 lbs: $175	$175-$300
Frontier	$20	$30	3+: $50	51+ lbs: $75	$75
Hawaiian	$25/$23 inter-island: $10	$35/$32 $17 inter-island: $17	3-6: $125 7+: $200 inter-island: $25	51-70 lbs: $50 inter-island: $25	$100 inter-island: $25
Jet Blue	$0	$30	3: $75	51-70 lbs: $50 71-100 lbs: $100	$75
Midwest	$20	$30	3+: $50	51-100 lbs: $75	$75

Table 3. (Continued)

Airline	First bag (airport/online)	Second bag (airport/online)	Additional bags (each)	Overweight bags	Oversized bags
Southwest	$0	$0	3-9: $50 10+: $110	51-100 lbs: $50	$50
Spirit[b]	$25/$19	$25	3-5: $100	51-70 lbs: $50 71-99 lbs: $100	$100-$150
Sun Country	$25/$20	$35/$30	$75	51-100 lbs: $75	$75
United[c]	$25	$35	3+: $100	51-100 lbs: $100	$100
USA3000	$25/$15	$25	$25	51-70 lbs: $25	$25-$50
US Airways	$25/$23	$35/$32	3-9: $100	51-70 lbs: $50 71-100 lbs: $100	$100
Virgin America	$25	$25	3-10: $25	1st <70 lbs: free 51-70 lbs: $50 71-100 lbs: $100	$50

Source: GAO review of airline Web Sites and interviews with airline officials.

[a] Alaska Airlines does not charge for the first 3 checked bags for trips wholly within the state of Alaska.

[b] Spirit revised its checked baggage fee for travel on or after August 1, 2010 to $25 for each of the first two bags, and $85 for each of the 3rd, 4th and 5th bags.

[c] United also offers a $249 annual fee to check one or two bags per flight without charge.

Table 4. Other Airline-Imposed Fees of 17 Airlines as of July 1, 2010

Airline	Ticket change or cancellation (domestic ticket)	Booking phone/ in person	Unaccompanied minor	Pet in cabin	Seat selection	Inflight food and beverage	Blanket and pillow
Air Tran	$75	$15/$0	$39 direct/non-stop $59 connecting	$69	$6 advance $20 exit row	F: NA B: $6	NA
Alaska	$100 ($75 online)	$15/$15	$25 direct/non-stop $50 connecting	$100	NA	F: $3.50-$7 B: $6	NA
Allegiant	$50 per segment	$15+$14.99 per segment /$0	NA	NA	$4.99-$24.99 varies by flight length and seat.	F: $2-$5 B: $2-$7[a]	NA
American	$150	$20/$20-$30	$100	$100	NA	F: $3-$10 B: $6-$7	$8
Continental	$150	$20/$20	$100	$125	NA	F: $0 B: $6	NA
Delta	$150	$20/$35	$100	$125	NA	F: $2-$8 B: $5-$7	NA
Frontier	$50 - $100	$0/$0	$50 direct/non-stop $100 connecting	$75	$15-$25	F: $3-$7 B: $2-$5[a]	NA
Hawaiian	$100-150 inter-island: $25-$30	$25/$35 inter-island: $15/$35	$100 inter-island: $35	$175	NA	F: $5.50-$10 B: $6.50-$14	NA
Jet Blue	$100	$15	$75	$100	$10 extra legroom	F: $0 B: $6	$7
Midwest	$100	$0/$0	$50 direct/non-stop $100 connecting	$75	NA	F: $3-$7 B: $2-$5[a]	NA

Table 4. (Continued)

Airline	Ticket change or cancellation (domestic ticket)	Booking phone/ in person	Unaccompanied minor	Pet in cabin	Seat selection	Inflight food and beverage	Blanket and pillow
Southwest	$0	$0/$0	$50	$75	$10 priority boarding	F: $0 B: $3-$5	NA
Spirit	$110 ($100 online)	$5/$0 ($5 each way online)	$100	$100	Varies based on location.	F: $2-$5 B: $2-$6[a]	NA
Sun Country	$75	$15/$0	$75/segment	$100	$8	F: $3-$6 B: $5	$5
United	$150	$25/$30	$99	$125	$9/$109	F: $3-$9 B: $6	NA
USA3000	$75	$0/$0	$50	$75	$9-$25	n/a	NA
US Airways	$150	$25-$35	$100 (non-stop flights only)	$100	$5+ Varies by location.	F: $3-$7 B: $7-$8	$7
Virgin America	$100 ($75 online)	$15/$10	$75	$100	NA	F, B: $2-$10	$12

Source: GAO analysis

[a] Fee for some nonalcoholic beverages.

APPENDIX III: COMMENTS FROM THE U.S. DEPARTMENT OF HOMELAND SECURITY

U.S. Department of Homeland Security
Washington, DC 20528

Homeland Security

July 9, 2010

Mr. Gerald L. Dillingham, Ph.D.
Director, Physical Infrastructure
U.S. Government Accountability Office
441 G Street, N.W.
Washington, DC 20548

Dear Dr. Dillingham:

RE: Draft Report GAO-10-785 (Reference # 540204), Commercial Aviation: Consumers Could Benefit From Better Information about Airline-Imposed Fees and Refund of Government-Imposed Taxes and Fees

Thank you for the opportunity to review the draft report concerning the Department of Homeland Security's (DHS) aviation taxes, fees, and surcharges. DHS concurs with GAO's report findings and proposed recommendation. DHS had one recommendation for executive action. We would like to respectfully offer the following comments:

GAO Recommendation: That the Secretary of Homeland Security determines whether a passenger is eligible for a refund of the customs and immigration inspection fees and provide this information to DOT, to eliminate ambiguity of government imposed fees that are eligible for refund to purchasers of unused nonrefundable tickets.

DHS Response: DHS concurs with this recommendation. DHS appreciates the follow-up teleconference call with GAO to discuss the Draft Report and also acknowledges the changes made by GAO in its revised sections of the report.

DHS has reviewed the revised sections of the Draft Report. CBP would like to note that there is no separate ICE fee as referred to in the revised sections. CBP collects and administers the immigration fee and transfers part of the collections to ICE. CBP recommends changing this language throughout the report. CBP also recommends that GAO use the same language in Table 2 for the Immigration fee that they use for the Customs fee.

Thank you for the opportunity to comment on this draft report and we look forward to working with you on future homeland security issues.

Sincerely,

Jerald E. Levine
Director
Departmental Audit Liaison Office

End Notes

[1] In this report, references to airlines are specific to U.S. passenger airlines, unless otherwise noted.

[2] We chose these 17 U.S. passenger airlines based on several factors. All 17 airlines report annual operating revenues of at least $20 million and together collected more than 99 percent of the checked baggage fees reported to BTS in 2008 and transported about 77 percent of domestic revenue passengers in 2008.

[3] This covers only passenger airlines with revenues of at least $20 million annually.

[4] Charging fees for services is also known as unbundling of charges, offering a la carte pricing, or charging ancillary fees.

[5] The three main GDSs are Amadeus, Sabre, and Travelport, which combined generated more than $9.6 billion in revenue in 2008.

[6] The full-fare advertising rule states "[t]he [Civil Aeronautics] Board considers any advertising or solicitation by a direct air carrier, indirect air carrier, or an agent of either, for passenger air transportation, a tour (i.e., a combination of air transportation and ground accommodations), or a tour component (e.g., a hotel stay) that states a price for such air transportation, tour, or tour component to be an unfair or deceptive practice, unless the price stated is the entire price to be paid by the customer to the air carrier, or agent, for such air transportation, tour, or tour component." 14 C.F.R. § 399.84. Through 25 years of enforcement case precedent, DOT has permitted carriers and ticket agents to separately state government taxes and fees imposed on a per passenger basis, such as passenger facility charges and international departure taxes, so long as their existence and amounts are disclosed clearly at the first point in an advertisement where a fare is presented. See e.g., United Airlines, Order 2009-8-17 (Aug. 25, 2009). See also 14 C.F.R. § 399.84 and 49 U.S.C. § 41712.

[7] Fuel charges must be included in the advertised fare; they cannot be stated separately. If they are stated separately, it violates the full-fare advertising rule. See 14 C.F.R. § 399.84 and 49 U.S.C. § 41712. DOT Guidance, *Prohibition of Deceptive Practices in the Marketing of Airfare to the Public Using the Internet*, (Jan. 18, 2001). See also Condor Flugdienst GmbH Consent Order, Order 2009-4-1 (Apr. 1, 2009).

[8] DOT, *Guidance on Disclosure of Policies and Charges Associated with Checked Baggage*, 73 Fed. Reg. 28854 (May 19, 2008).

[9] 14 C.F.R. § 234.6. Reports are required of an air carrier certificated under 49 U.S.C. § 41102 that accounted for at least 1 percent of domestic scheduled passenger revenues in the 12 months ending March 31 of each year, as reported to the Department pursuant to part 241 of this title. 14 C.F.R. § 234.2. A mishandled baggage report is a report filed with a carrier by or on behalf of a passenger that claims loss, delay, damage, or pilferage of baggage. 14 C.F.R. § 234.2.

[10] 14 C.F.R. § 254.4. This section applies to any flight segment using a large aircraft, or on any flight segment that is included on the same ticket as another flight segment that uses large aircraft. A large aircraft is defined as an aircraft designed to have a maximum passenger capacity of more than 60 seats. 14 C.F.R. § 254.3. This is also applicable only to domestic flights. This monetary limit is recalculated every 2 years based on the CPI-U. 14 C.F.R. § 254.6. Baggage liability requirements for all flights to and from the United States. are established in the Montreal Convention.

[11] Per 49 U.S.C. § 329(e)(2), the Secretary of Transportation may request that the Secretary of Homeland Security periodically report on the number of complaints about security screening.

[12] 26 U.S.C. § 4261(a). Taxable transportation is defined as transportation by air which begins and ends in the United States or in a 225-mile zone into Canada and Mexico from the

continental United States. 26 U.S.C. § 4262. Throughout we refer to this as domestic air transportation.

[13] 26 U.S.C. § 4261(b). The domestic segment tax is a flat tax based on the number of segments traveled and is not a percentage of amounts paid for transportation.

[14] 26 U.S.C. § 4261(c). Section 4261(c)(3) provides a modified international arrival/departure tax rate of $8.10 for segments that begin or end in Alaska or Hawaii (applies only to departures). The domestic segment tax and international arrival/departure tax are annually adjusted for inflation. Amounts listed are current for 2010.

[15] 49 U.S.C. § 44940, 49 C.F.R. part 1510. TSA began imposing this fee in February 2002.

[16] Immigration inspection fees are divided between CBP and ICE. Agricultural inspection fees are divided between CBP and USDA. According to the interagency agreements, fees are intended to be distributed among the agencies according to the cost of the activities for which the agencies are responsible.

[17] Elite members accumulate a specified minimum number of miles flown in a year or have surpassed a specified lifetime threshold.

[18] DOT Research and Innovative Technology Administration Bureau of Transportation Statistics Accounting and Reporting Directive, No. 289, February 20, 2009. DOT includes the sale of frequent flyer award program miles as ancillary revenues whereas we are reporting on revenues only from airline-imposed fees paid by passengers.

[19] For example, according to economic literature, alcoholic beverages are usually subject to two state-level taxes: an excise tax that is included in the shelf price and a sales tax that is applied at the cash register. Thus, the impact of an increase in the excise tax is likely to be more visible to the consumer than an increase in the sales tax. One study analyzed whether price visibility affected consumer demand and found that it did. Consumer demand was found to be far more responsive to changes in the more visible excise taxes than to changes in the less visible sales taxes. A similar study of purchases of household products found that applying sales taxes at the cash register rather than including them in shelf prices had a smaller impact on consumer demand. In this study, for some products in some stores, the analysts posted tags on the shelf showing the products' prices inclusive of the sales taxes and found that making the full prices visible reduced purchases of the products compared to other products, and the same products in other stores, that did not have their prices similarly tagged. (These studies are discussed more fully in Raj Chetty, Adam Looney, and Kory Kroft, "Salience and Taxation: Theory and Evidence," *American Economic Review*, 99, (2009): 1145-1177).

[20] In 2010, legislation was introduced that would require the Secretary of Transportation to complete a rulemaking prohibiting carriers from charging for carry-on baggage that falls within the restrictions imposed by the carrier with respect to size, weight, and number of bags. S. 3195, 111th Cong. (2010). Additionally, legislation was introduced to subject carry-on baggage fees to the 7.5 percent excise tax imposed on transportation of persons by air. S. 3205, 111th Cong. (2010).

[21] See 14 C.F.R. § 399.84 and 49 U.S.C. § 41712. Fuel charges must be included in the advertised fare; they cannot be stated separately. Stating them separately would violate the full-fare advertising rule and 49 U.S.C. § 41712. DOT Guidance, *Prohibition of Deceptive Practices in the Marketing of Airfare to the Public Using the Internet*, January 18, 2001. See also Condor Flugdienst GmbH Consent Order, Order 2009-4-1 (April 1, 2009). Although DOT's enforcement policy has been to consider "ticket agents," as defined in title 49, subject to the full-fare advertising rule, which on its face applies to "direct and indirect air carriers as well as 'an agent of either,'" DOT's recently-proposed rule would specifically name "ticket agents" as being covered by the rule. DOT, *Enhancing Airline Passenger Protections*, Notice of Proposed Rulemaking (NPRM), 75 Fed. Reg. 32318 (proposed June 8, 2010). According to DOT, this is because the statutory definition of "ticket agent" encompasses entities, in addition to agents of carriers that hold out, sell, or arrange for air transportation. See 49 U.S.C. § 40102(40).

[22] See DOT, *Guidance on Disclosure of Policies and Charges Associated with Checked Baggage*, 73 Fed. Reg. 28854 (May 19, 2008).

[23] See *Guidance on Disclosure of Policies and Charges Associated with Checked Baggage*, 73 Fed. Reg. 28854 (May 19, 2008), and 14 C.F.R. § 399.84.

[24] Clear Airfares Act of 2009, S. 2823, 111th Cong. § 2 (2009). See also S. 3195, 111th Cong. (2010).

[25] S. 3195, 111th Cong. (2010).

[26] DOT, *Enhancing Airline Passenger Protections,* NPRM, 75 Fed. Reg. 32318 (proposed June 8, 2010). The comment period closes August 9, 2010. In this context, DOT is seeking comment on whether this requirement should be limited to disclosure of "significant fees" for optional services, including the definition of "significant fee" and whether it should be defined as a particular dollar amount. Comment is also sought on alternatives to this option. DOT is also seeking comment as to whether this provision, proposed 14 C.F.R. § 399.85(c), should apply to ticket agents, as defined in 49 U.S.C. § 40102.

[27] DOT, *Enhancing Airline Passenger Protections*, NPRM, 75 Fed. Reg. 32318 (proposed June 8, 2010).

[28] DOT, *Enhancing Airline Passenger Protections*, NPRM, 75 Fed. Reg. 32318 (proposed June 8, 2010).

[29] IRS determinations of the applicability of the 7.5 percent excise tax depend on the facts and circumstances pertaining to the imposition of the fee and, accordingly, may vary from airline to airline for similar services.

[30] IRS guidance includes Revenue Rulings, Private Letter Rulings, and other guidance documents.

[31] 26 U.S.C. § 4261(a). 26 U.S.C. § 9502.

[32] 26 C.F.R. §§ 49.4261-7, 49.4261-8.

[33] See Rev. Rul. 73-508, 1973-2, C.B. 366.

[34] See Rev. Rul. 80-31, 1980-1, C.B. 251.

[35] A Revenue Ruling is an official interpretation by the IRS of the internal revenue laws and related statutes, treaties, and regulations as applied to a specific set of facts. They are issued for the information and guidance of taxpayers; published revenue rulings may be cited as precedent by the IRS. Private Letter Rulings are taxpayer-specific rulings furnished by the IRS in response to requests made by taxpayers. Since it is taxpayer specific, it cannot be used or cited as precedent.

[36] See 26 C.F.R. § 49.4261-8; Rev. Rul. 80-31; Priv. Ltr. Rul. 118216-09 (Sept. 28, 2009).

[37] See 26 C.F.R. § 49.4261-7; Rev. Rul. 89-109, 1989-2 C.B. 232; Rev. Rul. 73-508, 1973; Priv. Ltr. Rul. 118216-09.

[38] Because U.S. airlines charge fees for overweight and oversize bags as well as for additional bags, these fees are included in the $2.5 billion. In fiscal year 2007, before U.S. airlines began charging for first and second checked bags, airlines reported $457 million in baggage fee revenues.

[39] For this analysis, we are making the simplifying assumption that the additional tax due would not have caused any passengers to choose not to purchase tickets. Any such reduction in purchases would presumably have been small and would have had the effect of making the increase in taxes collected a little smaller than our estimate. This figure is also based on total baggage fee revenues, including international baggage fees that would presumably not be subject to the 7.5 percent excise tax. If only the portion of baggage fees collected for domestic air transportation had been subject to the excise tax in fiscal year 2009, the estimate of additional amounts credited to the Trust Fund would be smaller. The reported data do not allow us to identify the portion of baggage fee revenues collected on international flights. However, since most travelers on international flights are permitted to check one or two bags at no additional charge as long as they do not exceed a specified weight requirement, we believe that this portion is small and the impact of including these fee revenues is correspondingly small.

[40] In April 2010, a bill was introduced that would subject revenues from bags carried on to the aircraft to the 7.5 percent excise tax, as an amount paid for taxable transportation. Block Airlines' Gratuitous Fees Act, or the "BAG Fees Act," S. 3205, 111th Cong. (2010).

[41] 26 C.F.R. part 49, subpart D.

[42] It is unknown whether baggage fees have had an effect on the rate of mishandled baggage per thousand bags as this information is not available.

[43] U.S. passenger airlines that have at least 1 percent of total domestic scheduled service passenger revenues are required to file monthly reports of mishandled baggage with DOT. 14 C.F.R. §§ 234.6, 234.2.

[44] A contract of carriage is an agreement between a passenger and an airline that encompasses all contractual rights, liabilities, and duties of the two parties. Any term or condition of this contract is legally binding on the airline and the passenger and may be enforced in the courts. Checked baggage is also handled by TSA staff which conduct security screening. TSA has its own liability and claims review process that is different from airlines and which follows the Federal Tort Claims Act and related Department of Justice regulations. According to the Act and regulations, the government's liability and actual damages are generally determined by state tort law and a customer must make a claim within 2 years of the loss. 28 U.S.C. § 2401(b); 28 C.F.R. part 14. TSA and airlines attempted to reach an agreement on processing mishandled baggage claims, however, because of differences in claims processing, that attempt was unsuccessful.

[45] Although the 10 U.S. airlines' contracts of carriage did not say whether they provide bag delivery, the airlines may do so, but not make that service part of the contracts.

[46] 14 C.F.R. § 254.4. Per regulation, this amount is reviewed by DOT every two years and adjusted in accordance with the Consumer Price Index. 14 C.F.R. § 254.6. DOT regulations also require notice of this limitation to be provided to passengers. 14 C.F.R. § 254.5.

[47]DOT prescribes what a contract of carriage should generally include, for example, incorporation by reference terminology, which is permissive but not prescriptive. 14 C.F.R. part 253.

[48] DOT, *Guidance on Reimbursement of Passenger Expenses Incurred as a Result of Lost, Damaged, or Delayed Baggage*, October 9, 2009. The letter further explained that to meet the requirements of Part 254 and the requirements implicit in 49 U.S.C. § 41712, carriers should remain willing to cover all reasonable, actual and verifiable expenses related to baggage loss, damage or delay up to the amount stated in Part 254. DOT took enforcement action against Spirit Airlines in September 2004 in part for limiting its delayed bag expense reimbursement to roundtrip passengers and expenses after the first 24 hours. Order 2009-9-8 (Sept. 17, 2009).

[49] DOT, *Enhancing Airline Passenger Protections*, NPRM, 75 Fed. Reg. 32318 (proposed June 8, 2010). The NPRM also proposes to require carriers to include a provision in their Customer Service Plans to make every reasonable effort to return mishandled bags within 24 hours, to compensate passengers for reasonable expenses that result from delay in delivery, and to include customer service plans in their contract of carriage.

[50] FAA's Carry-on Baggage Rule, 14 C.F.R. § 121.589, does not set forth specific limitations on the number of bags or items a passenger can bring on to an aircraft; rather, it requires air carriers to have an approved carry-on baggage program in place.

[51] Survey of Flight Attendants, Association of Flight Attendants, February 2010. The results we cite are only representative of the 800 responding flight attendants.

[52] 49 C.F.R. § 1510.9(b). Letter from Randall Fiertz, Transportation Security Administration, Acting Director of Revenue, to James Hultquist, Air Transport Association, Managing Director, Taxes. November 21, 2002, Docket No. TSA-02-11120-59. TSA imposes $2.50 per enplanement not to exceed $5 one-way or $10 roundtrip for aviation security inspection services. 49 C.F.R. §§ 1510.9(b), 1510.5

[53] If a collecting airline refunds the TSA fee to a passenger, the airline, through Treasury, submits this "credit" along with the fees it has collected at the end of the month in which the fees

were collected, as required by statute. 49 U.S.C. § 44940(e)(3). The airline cannot retain any part of the fee to cover its costs; however, pursuant to statute, the airline is allowed to retain the interest earned from the trust account where fees are held. 49 U.S.C. § 44940(e)(6).

[54] Rev. Rul. 89-109 (1989) 1989-2, CB 232, as applicable to the 7.5 percent excise tax. IRS officials stated that the reasoning in this revenue ruling is also applicable to the passenger segment tax, and the international arrival/departure tax.

[55] 49 C.F.R. § 1510.9(b).

[56] The 17 U.S. passenger airlines are: Air Tran, Alaska Airlines, Allegiant Air, American Airlines, Continental Airlines, Delta Air Lines, Frontier Airlines, Hawaiian Airlines, JetBlue Airways, Midwest Airlines, Southwest Airlines, Spirit Airlines, Sun Country Airlines, United Airlines, US Airways, USA3000, and Virgin America. We chose these 17 airlines based on several factors. All 17 airlines reported annual operating revenues of at least $20 million and together collected more than 99 percent of the checked baggage fees reported to BTS in 2008 and transported about 77 percent of domestic revenue passengers in 2008. Two airlines—Virgin America and Spirit Airlines—did not respond to our request for information.

In: Commercial Airlines: Passenger Fee Issues ISBN: 978-1-61761-989-2
Editors: Michael J. Liguori

Chapter 2

HEARING ON "AIRLINE FEES", SUBCOMMITTEE ON AVIATION STAFF-JULY 12, 2010

Michael J. Liguori

PURPOSE OF THE HEARING

The Subcommittee on Aviation will meet on Wednesday, July 14, at 2:00 p.m., in room 2167 of the Rayburn House Office Building to receive testimony regarding airline fees. The hearing will cover a number of issues pertaining to the trend of unbundling airfares to require passengers to pay for particular services individually. The hearing will also explore requirements for disclosure of fares, taxes, and fees, options for passengers to recover the costs of some fees, and revenue potentially available to the Airport and Airway Trust Fund (Trust Fund) if certain ancillary fees were subject to the Federal tax on airline tickets.

BACKGROUND

From 2001 through 2009, the U.S. airline industry, including air cargo carriers, posted a cumulative net loss of $58.1 billion. Yearly industry-wide net losses, which were offset by modest profits in 2006-07, were the result of many factors, including the aftermath of the September 11, 2001, terrorist attacks, the SARS epidemic, excess capacity, record oil prices of up to $147 per barrel, and an economic recession. According to an airline association, high fuel prices, in particular, have created persistently challenging conditions. From January to April of 2010, U.S. airlines paid 26.8 percent more for jet fuel than in the same period of 2009.[1]

Starting in mid 2007, in response to these economic challenges, many airlines began to unbundle services by instituting separate fees for checked baggage. Airlines next introduced "a la carte" fees for passenger services, some of which traditionally have been considered as included in the cost of a ticket. By the end of 2009, airlines charged for numerous ancillary services, including seat selection, extra leg room, beverages, meals, and more.

According to the BTS, U.S. airlines collected a total of $7.8 billion in ancillary fees in 2009,[2] including $2.7 billion in baggage fees alone. In the fourth quarter of 2009, U.S. airlines collected 18.3 percent more in ancillary revenue than in the fourth quarter of 2008. Collectively, U.S. passenger airlines incurred $5.5 billion in operating losses in 2008, but reported operating profits of approximately $1.2 billion in 2009.[3]

The proliferation of ancillary fees over a relatively short period of time has raised concerns over the costs and transparency of such fees. Often, consumers are not entirely aware of the range of fees that they may encounter in the ticket booking process, at check-in, and at the gate. A recent poll conducted by Consumer Reports of consumers on what "annoys travelers the most," luggage charges and added fees rated the highest, at 8.4 and 8.1, respectively, based on a 10 point scale.[4]

I. Nature of Ancillary Fees

It is estimated that airlines present passengers with more than 100 ancillary fee options in the course of travel. The table below provides a description of items and services for which some airlines currently charge ancillary fees. The actual fees charged vary widely depending on each individual airline's policies.

Although critics have suggested that ancillary fees are merely a means for airlines to "nickel- and-dime" passengers, the Air Transport Association (ATA) maintains that ancillary fee policies are beneficial to passengers because such policies allow passengers to pay only for services that they use.

In addition, the ATA states that many airlines offer "restricted" tickets, which are less expensive but carry greater fees and penalties for changes to itineraries, as opposed to "full-fare" tickets, which allow changes free of additional charge. ATA argues that this price difference allows the cost of air travel to remain much lower for consumers who do not make changes to their itineraries.[5]

In addition to ancillary fees levied by airlines, the Federal Government imposes direct taxes and fees on passengers for their ticket purchase. Some of these fees vary according to each traveler's itinerary.

Ancillary Fees Charged by Airlines

Baggage	Ticketing	In-Flight Services
1st Checked Bag	Change or Cancellation	Food
2nd Checked Bag	Booking (phone/in person/online)	Beverage
Additional Bags	Unaccompanied Minors	Blankets
Overweight Bags	Pets	Pillows
Oversized Bags	Seat Selection (location, additional legroom, exit row)	Wireless Internet
	Early Boarding	In-flight entertainment
	Holiday Travel Surcharge	Misc. (e.g., antlers, firearms, extra seats for overweight passengers)
	Fuel Surcharge	
	Standby	
	Frequent Flyer Redemption	
	Club Membership	

In addition, airports may also impose a passenger facility charge (PFC) of up to $4.50 per flight segment.

For nonrefundable tickets that are unused by the passenger, the question has been raised as to whether government taxes and fees can be refunded to the passenger. According to the GAO, the 7.5 percent passenger ticket tax is generally not refundable. In addition, it is not always clear to the passenger whether other government taxes and fees are refundable and, if they are, how the passenger can obtain a refund.

Government-Imposed Taxes on Passengers[6]

Government Tax or Fee	Amount and Description
Passenger Ticket Tax	7.5 percent: A tax levied as a percentage of the fare that the passenger pays for a domestic airline ticket.
Flight Segment Tax	$3.70 per flight segment: Paid by the passenger based on the number of segments in the passenger's itinerary for domestic travel. A segment is single flight from a takeoff to landing. This tax is not applicable to passengers departing from rural airports.[7]
Alaska/Hawaii Ticket Tax and Facilities Tax	7.5 percent: A tax imposed on passengers on domestic flights to or from Alaska or Hawaii. $8.10 is also charged for any ticket not subject to the ticket tax.
Frequent Flyer Award Tax	7.5 percent: A tax on amounts paid by companies with frequent flyer marketing arrangements with airlines (including credit card companies).
International Departure/ Arrival Tax	$16.10: Imposed on passengers on international flights departing or arriving in the United States.
September 11 Security Fee	$2.50: Funds the Transportation Security Administration at up to $5 per one-way trip and $10 per round trip
U.S. Customs Fee	$5.50: Funds inspections by U.S. Customs. Assessed for travel on tickets issued to passengers arriving from outside the U.S. Customs territory.
Immigration Fee	$7.00: Assessed for travel from any international point into the United States.
Agricultural Inspection Fee	$5.00: Assessed for travel from any international point into the United States and Puerto Rico. Funds agricultural quarantine and inspection.

II. Revenue

According to the GAO, airlines have reported a four-fold increase from 2008 to 2009 in revenue from ancillary fees. However, the GAO notes that precise comparisons are difficult, because airlines report ancillary revenue from fees other than baggage fees differently. In 2008, checked baggage revenue was reported to be $1.1 billion. For 2009, airlines collected $2.7 billion from baggage fees, $2.4 billion from reservation change fees, and $2.7 billion from other ancillary fees. The table below shows ancillary revenues by airline, ranked by the total amount collected in 2009.

In terms of ancillary fee revenue as a percentage of total operating revenue for 2009, Spirit reported the highest with 20 percent of operating revenue from fees, followed by AirTran at 10.7 percent, Allegiant at 10 percent, Delta at 9.1 percent, and US Airways at 8.5 percent.[8]

Ancillary fees and the associated revenues they generate have prompted some policymakers to question whether such fees should be subject to the 7.5 percent tax on airline tickets, especially if the services provided for such fees were traditionally included in base ticket prices. The Internal Revenue Code imposes a 7.5 percent excise tax on the amount a passenger pays for "taxable transportation"[9] – essentially, the passenger's airline ticket. Certain airline charges, however, are not taxable; Federal regulations (last amended in 1962) exclude, from the excise tax, fees for "transportation of baggage" as well as fees for "nontransportation services," among others.[10]

Last year, the Internal Revenue Service (IRS) issued a private letter ruling,[11] which stated that an ancillary fee is subject to the excise tax only if it is "paid as a condition to receiving air transportation" and is not paid for an "optional" service that is "not reasonably necessary to the air transportation itself."[12] The IRS concluded that fees for the following services are not subject to the excise tax: checked baggage, headsets for use with in-flight entertainment systems, food and alcoholic beverages in flight, and ticket changes.

Airlines' Ancillary Fee Revenue (in millions of dollars)

Airline	4th Quarter 2008	4th Quarter 2009	Percent Change 4Q 2008-4Q 2009 (%)	Total 2009 Ancillary Fee Revenue
Delta	289.0	425.7	47.3	1,647.6
American	246.2	253.3	2.9	1,002.4
US Airways	227.0	231.8	2.1	912.1
Northwest	185.2	156.7	-15.4	718.7
United	151.3	146.2	-3.4	619.5
Southwest	140.6	157.2	11.8	617.1
Continental	77.5	129.1	66.6	539.7
AirTran	36.2	61.2	69.1	249.7
JetBlue	49.5	48.1	-2.8	193.1
Alaska	30.2	42.2	39.7	147.0
Industry Total	**1,615.1**	**1,911.1**	**18.3**	**7,825.7**

Source: BTS, Form 41; Schedule P1.2.

The Trust Fund – the source of money for the Federal Aviation Administration's (FAA) capital programs to maintain and improve airports and facilities, and for some FAA operations – draws revenue from excise taxes such as the tax on passenger tickets.[13] At a time when the FAA's primary fund for capital programs is in decline, a hypothetical application of the 7.5 percent tax to ancillary fees could generate additional revenue for necessary aviation programs. In 2009, the GAO found that, if the Trust Fund's uncommitted cash balance fell below $752 million (its then-forecast balance), the "decline . . . could pose budgetary challenges for FAA."[14] At the end of calendar year 2009, however, the Trust Fund's uncommitted cash balance had fallen to $299 million, according to information provided by FAA officials to staff.

Adding ancillary fees to the taxable charges that arise as part of air transportation could increase the Trust Fund's balance.[15] Based on BTS data, if all baggage fees charged in 2009[16] had been subject to the tax, Trust Fund revenue would have increased by approximately $202.5 million, assuming all other factors (including demand) remained constant. That revenue would have represented a roughly 1.1 percent increase in Trust Fund income from excise taxes in 2009, according to FAA-provided data.

III. Legal Requirements for Disclosures of Fees: Current and Proposed

As the number of fees charged by airlines grows increasingly complex, with requirements for disclosure not yet updated to reflect the pricing changes, consumers are oftentimes left confused about what they will really pay for the total cost of their travel itinerary. The Department of Transportation's (DOT) Office of Aviation Enforcement and Proceedings is responsible for economic regulation of airlines and for protecting consumers.

A. Current Law

1. Full Fare Advertising Rule

By statute, airlines may not engage in unfair or deceptive practices when advertising airfares.[17] In 1984, the DOT adopted the "full fare advertising rule." Under the rule, an advertisement that states an airfare advertisement is "an unfair or deceptive practice, unless the price stated is the entire price to be paid by the customer to the air carrier, or agent, for such air transportation."[18]

The Secretary of Transportation has authority to investigate violations of these requirements and to assess a civil penalty of up to $2,500 for each violation.[19]

The DOT interprets the rule to permit an airline to disclose government taxes and fees separately from the base fare quoted in an advertisement, but only if, among other things, the taxes and fees are levied or approved by a government agency and the advertisement, on its face, clearly indicates the amounts of such taxes and fees, so that the prospective passenger can calculate the total cost of travel.[20] An Internet advertisement that, on the customer's first encounter, merely displays a certain fare "plus taxes/fees," without specifying the amounts of those taxes and fees or directing the customer to another page that lists their amounts, does not comply with these requirements.[21]

Through various rulings and guidance, the DOT has required that airlines and ticket agents disclose the following fees in airfare advertisements: fuel surcharges, peak travel and holiday surcharges, and government fees, among others.

2. Baggage and Change Fees

In May 2008, in response to the growing trend of airlines levying fees for checked baggage (which traditionally were not levied for up to two bags of up to 50-70 pounds), the DOT issued guidance on disclosure of policies and charges associated with checked baggage, by stating:

> The [DOT's] long-standing policy has been to require carriers to clearly disclose significant conditions applicable to air fares. Failure to disclose such conditions has been considered an unfair and deceptive practice and unfair method of competition. . . . [and DOT] considers such significant conditions to include limiting passengers to fewer than two free checked bags of the size and weight that have generally been free on the carrier in the past and to assessing passengers a charge in addition to the air fare for such checked baggage.[22]

The guidance requires that airlines disclose baggage fees and baggage policies in Internet advertising "on the first screen in which the carrier offers a fare quotation of a specific itinerary selected by the customer," and it requires disclosure of the baggage fee in close proximity to the fare for print advertising. Similarly, airline reservation agents must disclose fees during telephone and counter sales.

B. Proposed Rulemaking

The DOT recently issued a notice of proposed rulemaking (NPRM) that includes both a number of proposed enhancements to existing consumer protections and poses a number of questions for comment. The NPRM expresses the DOT's conclusion that "there is a need to enhance protections for air travelers by establishing rules to ensure adequate notice of such fees for optional services to consumers . . . . Consumers are not always made aware of the extra charges that a carrier may impose . . . [including] services that traditionally been included in the ticket price."[23]

To address these issues and to help passengers determine the full price of air travel (the airfare, which includes government taxes and fees, plus ancillary fees for services), the NPRM solicits public comments on whether *two prices* should be provided with respect to an advertised airfare: (1) ***full fare***, including all mandatory charges (i.e., anything the passenger must pay to fly); and (2) "***full fare-plus***," which DOT tentatively proposes to mean the full fare plus baggage fees and fees for carry-on items (the costs of which were traditionally included in ticket prices).

The DOT is seeking comment on whether the second price – the "full fare-plus" – should include all services that traditionally have been included in the prices of the ticket, as opposed to just those services relating to the transport of baggage, and what exactly such services would include. In the alternative, the DOT is seeking comment on whether sellers of air transportation should be required to display on their Web sites information regarding optional fees selected by the passenger when conducting a query and information on the passenger's "full price," which would be tailored based each passenger's indication of his or her needs.

The DOT further proposes to amend its current price advertising rule to prohibit carriers and ticket agents from automatically including "opt-out" provisions in price advertising. According to the NPRM, the DOT has found that some sellers of airline tickets add, into the total price of air transportation, fees for ancillary services, which the consumer "is deemed to have accepted unless he or she affirmatively opts out of the service and related charges."[24] These optional fees, for items such as seat selection, are preselected for the passenger and added to the total fare, without the passenger affirmatively selecting the add-on.

Additionally, the DOT's NPRM proposes to require carriers to disclose all applicable fees, including those for ancillary services, through a prominent link on each carrier's Web site that leads to a listing of all fees for optional services.

The NPRM also indicates the DOT may require carriers to provide up-to-date, comprehensive fee information to the operators of Internet Web sites that sell airline tickets and to travel and ticket agents. It is estimated that at least half of all airline tickets in the United States are sold by travel agencies. In a recent letter to the DOT, two organizations that represent ticket agents and global distribution systems (GDSs)[25] stated, "The critical problem that remains is the practical inability of travel agencies to obtain from each airline on whose behalf they sell tickets the needed baggage and other ancillary fee information in a usable, reliable and efficient manner."[26] In response to this issue, the DOT has indicated that it is considering whether to require carriers to make ancillary fee information available to GDSs. The current system through which airlines provide fare information to ticket agents and GDSs is administered by the Airline Tariff Publishing Company (ATPCO), which has developed a new database system for ancillary fees with more than 100 unique fields for airlines to input information on their specific fees.

Many airlines oppose a mandate to provide GDS companies with access to information on optional services and pricing because they believe it would place airlines at a competitive disadvantage in the marketplace, further strengthen GDS market power, thwart the entry of new competitors in the GDS market, and expose consumers to higher prices necessary to recoup GDSs' fees.

The proposal also seeks to require each carrier that issues electronic ticket confirmations to passengers to include information on the carrier's baggage fee policies. The DOT believes these requirements will ensure that passengers avoid unexpected baggage charges at the airport and will save time for airline personnel and passengers at the airport.

IV. The Future of Ancillary Fees

Ancillary fees – a newfound source of significant revenue for airlines in a challenging marketplace – are still a fairly new concept for the airline industry and are constantly evolving. The DOT, consumer groups, GDSs, airlines themselves, and industry stakeholders are working to make fees more transparent for consumers. For example, the Institute of Travel and Meetings recently announced the formation of a group to set standards and policies for airlines regarding product unbundling. [27] An airline consulting firm recently proposed a "passenger bill of rights" on a la carte fees to provide passengers with greater transparency.[28] On June 8, 2010, the International Air Transport

Association (IATA) announced a new database called Automated Carrier Baggage Rules (ACBR) that will contain airlines' varying rules on baggage. IATA hopes the ACBR will enable airlines, travel agents, and passengers to better understand what baggage rules apply to any given itinerary, given that baggage rules have become "increasingly complex and confusing."[29]

Most industry analysts suggest that the nature and scope of airline fees may continue to expand. Airlines are still testing fees and consumer reactions to them. For example, US Airways instituted a fee for nonalcoholic beverages, but withdrew it after negative passenger reaction.

Industry analysts suggest that the next chapter of the story on ancillary fees will involve "rebundling" the fees into packages of options that the passenger can purchase in advance. There has also been discussion as to whether airlines will make the fees easier to refund when services are not actually delivered, and whether "elite" frequent flyers will be subjected to fewer ancillary fees. In addition, there is discussion about options available to passengers in purchasing ancillary fees. Under some concepts, for example, passengers may be able to pay for checked baggage in advance using GDSs. What is clear is that ancillary fees have generated revenue for the airline industry and will likely be the subject of regulation and continuing scrutiny.

Witnesses

Dr. Gerald Dillingham
Director of Civil Aviation Issues
U.S. Government Accountability Office

Mr. Robert S. Rivkin
General Counsel
U.S. Department of Transportation

Mr. Ben Baldanza
President and CEO
Spirit Airlines, Inc.

Mr. Dave Ridley
Senior Vice President
Marketing and Revenue Management
Southwest Airlines

Mr. Kevin Mitchell
Chairman
Business Travel Coalition

Mr. Kyle Moore
Vice President, Product Marketing
Sabre Travel Industry Group
and on behalf of
Interactive Travel Services Association
American Society of Travel Agents
Consumer Travel Alliance

End Notes

[1] Bureau of Transportation Statistics (BTS), *Airline Fuel Cost and Consumption (U.S. Carriers - Scheduled)*, http://www.transtats.bts.gov/fuel.asp.

[2] BTS' ion of ancillary fees includes: baggage fees, reservation change fees and miscellaneous operating revenue,definit including pet transportation, sale of frequent flyer award miles to airline business partners, and standby passenger fees. Revenue from seating assignments and on-board sales of food, drink, pillows, blankets, entertainment, or any other ancillary items are reported as Transport Related Revenue and cannot be identified separately.

[3] Source: BTS and the Government Accountability Office (GAO). Calculated based on operating losses for passenger airlines with revenues over $20 million, excluding cargo carriers.

[4] ConsumerReports.org, *Things That Annoy Travelers Most: Consumer Reports Survey Results*, www.consumerreports.org/cro/magazine-archive/2010/june/money/top-travel - gripes/overview/index.htm.

[5] ATA, *Airline Ancillary Revenues*, http://www.airlines. org/PublicPolicy/IssueBriefs/ Pages/AirlineAncillaryRevenues.aspx..

[6] See Airlines Reporting Corporation, *Industry Agents' Handbook, Taxes Fees and Charges*.

[7] A rural airport tax is levied at 7.5 percent on passengers whose flights depart or arrive at rural airports. This is assessed in lieu of the general passenger ticket tax. When the rural airport tax applies, there no segment fee is assessed.

[8] Press Release, BTS, *4th-Quarter 2009 Airline Financial Data: Low-Cost and Regional Airlines Report Profits, Network Carriers Report Loss* (May 3, 2010), http://www.bts.gov/ press_releases/2010/bts021_10/html/bts021_10.html.

[9] 26 U.S.C. § 4261(a) (2010).

[10] 26 C.F.R. §§ 49.4261-8(f)(1), (4) (2010).

[11] A private letter ruling is directed solely to the taxpayer who requests it and is limited to the facts as presented by that particular taxpayer; the ruling is not binding on other taxpayers and holds no precedential value. Whether or not the IRS would rule that ancillary fees are not taxable in all cases remains an unsettled question.

[12] IRS, Private Letter Ruling 118216-09 (Jan. 15, 2010), at 8.

[13] 26 U.S.C. § 9502(b) (2010).

[14] GAO, *Airline Industry Contraction Due to Volatile Fuel Prices and Falling Demand Affects Airports, Passengers, and Federal Government Revenues*, GAO-09-393 (April 2009), at 38.

[15] Unless otherwise indicated, all estimates discussed in this summary are based on data reported by the BTS. Estimates of tax revenue are the product of total reported fees multiplied by the 7.5 percent excise tax and do not account for variables such as changes in demand.

[16] Figures reported by the BTS. *See* BTS, *1st-Quarter 2010 Airline Financial Data: Low-Cost and Regional Airlines Report Profits, Network Carriers Report Loss,* Table 1A: "Baggage Fee Collections" (June 28, 2010), *http://www.bts.gov/press_releases/2010/bts031_10* /html/bts031_10.html.

[17] 49 U.S.C. § 41712(a) (2010).

[18] 14 C.F.R. § 399.84 (2010).

[19] *See* 49 U.S.C. §§ 41712, 46301 (2010).

[20] *See United Air Lines, Inc., Violations of 49 U.S.C. § 41712 and 14 C.F.R. § 399.84,* DOT Dkt. No. DOT-OST-2009-0001, Order No. 2009-8-17 (Aug. 25, 2009).

[21] *Id.; Spirit Airlines, Inc., Violations of 49 U.S.C. § 41712 and 14 C.F.R. § 399.84,* DOT Dkt. No. DOT-OST-2008-0031, Order No. 2008-12-14 (Dec. 23, 2008).

[22] DOT, *Guidance on Disclosure of Policies and Charges Associated with Checked Baggage,* 73 Fed. Reg. 28854 (May 19, 2008).

[23] Enhancing Airline Passenger Protections, 75 Fed. Reg. 32329 (June 8, 2010) (to be codified at 49 C.F.R. Part 399).

[24] *Id.* at 32328.

[25] A GDS generally refers to a computer reservation system that includes reservation databases of airlines. This term has largely replaced the term "computerized reservation system" (CRS).

[26] Letter from Paul M. Ruden, Senior Vice President, Legal and Industry Affairs, American Society of Travel Agents and Arthur B. Sackler, Executive Director, Interactive Travel Services Association to Sam Podberesky, Assistant General Counsel for Aviation Enforcement and Proceedings, DOT (Mar. 10, 2010).

[27] Jennifer Michels, "Industry Solutions Group Aims to Set Airline Unbundling Standards," *Aviation Daily* (Nov. 12, 2009).

[28] Andrew Compart, "Ancillary Revenue Conference Host Pushes for 'Bill,'' *Aviation Daily* (Nov. 24, 2009).

[29] IATA Press Release, *IATA Brings Transparency to Baggage Rules – New Simplifying the Business Project* (June 8, 2010).

In: Commercial Airlines: Passenger Fee Issues ISBN: 978-1-61761-989-2
Editors: Michael J. Liguori

Chapter 3

STATEMENT OF ROBERT S. RIVKIN, GENERAL COUNSEL, U.S. DEPARTMENT OF TRANSPORTATION, BEFORE THE SUBCOMMITTEE ON AVIATION, HEARING ON "AIRLINE FEES"

Chairman Costello, Ranking Member Petri and Members of the Subcommittee: I am pleased to appear before the Subcommittee today to discuss the U.S. Department of Transportation's commitment to vigorous compliance and enforcement efforts to protect the rights of airline passengers. I will emphasize steps taken by the Department to ensure that airline passengers have accurate and complete information about the full cost of the air transportation they are purchasing, including the ancillary airlines fees they must pay.

First, let me emphasize the importance Secretary LaHood and this Administration place on the rights of airline consumers. From the start, we have carefully examined our regulatory authority to determine how best to assist airline consumers with the most serious problems they face, including lengthy tarmac delays, chronically delayed flights, and lack of consumer information on the on-time performance of flights. We decided to add clear limits on tarmac delays, tough rules on chronically delayed flights and more disclosure to passengers than had been proposed in the prior administration's rulemaking we inherited. In December 2009, we took the most forceful regulatory action then available to us by issuing a rule including those provisions.

Recognizing that much more had to be done, after issuing our first consumer protection rule, we have now proposed more comprehensive regulatory protections. In June we issued a Notice of Proposed Rulemaking (NPRM) to strengthen the reforms enacted by our first rule—for example, to cover foreign carriers and more U.S. airports under our tarmac delay rule—and to deal with a number of other problems, most notably inadequate denied boarding compensation, deceptive air fare advertising, and insufficient disclosure of airline ancillary fees.

Because the topic of today's hearing is "airline fees", I will expand on the NPRM proposals designed to make it easier for consumers to know how much they will have to pay for airline transportation and ensure that airlines' fee-related practices are fair. First and foremost, the NPRM would require true full price advertising. Under the proposal advertised prices would be required to include all mandatory taxes, fees and charges. If the consumer has to pay the charge to fly, like a fuel surcharge, an excise tax, a travel agent service charge, or an internet ticket convenience fee, the charge would have to be included in the price presentation to each consumer.

Also, as we explain in the NPRM, we are skeptical that airlines should be allowed to label as "fares" prices that do not include numerous mandatory charges, and thusserve only to confuse or deceive consumers regarding the true full price of the ticket and to make price comparisons difficult. We have proposed to prohibit this misleadinglisting of fares .

Second, we propose that airline optional fees be fully disclosed on airline websites. By optional or ancillary fees, we mean charges for things like checking baggage or seat assignments that passengers can avoid but still fly. Our optional-fee-disclosure proposal results from what the Department feels is oftena lack of clear and adequate disclosure of these fees by airlines; consumers are not always able to determine the cost of their own travel (the ticket price plus the price of additional fees for optional services) prior to purchase.

Third, the NPRM would require more detailed and prominent disclosure for fees related to carry-on baggage and the first two pieces of checked baggage. For example, carriers would be required to issue e-ticket confirmations to passengers that include information regarding their free baggage allowance and/or the applicable fee for a carry-on bag or the first and second checked bag on the e-ticket confirmation. By providing this information to consumerson the e -ticket confirmation, passengers will be clearly informed well before the flight date and arrival at the airport of the applicable baggage rules and charges.

Fourth, we seek comment on the costs and benefits of requiring that two prices be provided in certain air fare advertising—the ticket price which is the full fare, including all mandatory charges, as well as that ticket price plus the cost of baggage charges that traditionally have been included in the price of the ticket, if these prices differ. We solicit comment on whether such a requirement for a second price, if adopted, should be limited to the full fare plus the cost of baggage charges or expanded to include other optional services that traditionally have been included in the priceof the ticket , such as obtaining seat assignments in advance.

Fifth, the Department is considering requiring airlines to provide their agents and global distribution systems—that is, computerized, online airline reservations systems like Amedeus thatdisplay multiple carrier offerings — complete, accurate, and up-to-date information on ancillary fees so that internet and store-front travel agents can provide that information to consumers.

Sixth, the NPRM seeks comment on the possibility of requiring sellers of air transportation to display on their websites comparative full fare information based on the ancillary service desires of a passenger. So if a customer wants to select a seat and check two bags on a flight from A to B on a specific date, the customer would see what the total price would be for each carrier providing the desired air transportation.

In addition to prohibiting deceptive fee advertising and disclosure, the new proposed rule also addresses fee reimbursement. It solicits comments on requiring carriers to reimburse passengers the fee charged to transport a bag if that bag is not timely delivered and explains that, when a flight is cancelled, carriers must refund not only the ticket price but also any optional fees charged to a passenger for that flight (e.g., baggage fees, "service charges" for use of frequent flyer miles when the flight is canceled by the carrier).

The comment period on the NPRM is currently scheduled to close on August 9, 2010, although we have recently receiveda request to extend the comment period. We have set an aggressive timeline and hope to complete our rulemaking by the end of the year.

Our wide-ranging rulemaking activities have not detracted from an expansion of our aviation compliance and enforcementwork. For example, over the past two years our Aviation Enforcement Office has conducted 16 on-site investigations at airline headquarters to measure their compliance with our existing passenger rights regulations. Five of those investigations have already resulted in cease and desist orders assessing large airlines almost $1.2 million in civil penalties, primarily related to violations of our denied boarding compensation requirements. The other investigations may result in similar enforcement actions. More important perhaps than the resulting enforcement actions, these on-site visits emphasize to carriers their responsibilities and foster future compliance.

Another significant enforcement activity focuses on deceptive airline and agent fare advertising. During the year ending June 30, 2010, the Department issued 11 cease and desist orders assessing $520,000 in civil penalties in cases involving deceptive advertising alone. Three other orders covered deceptive advertising as well as other issues.

In the past year we also issued our first enforcement orders related to lengthy tarmac delays. Specifically, the Department levied a total of $175,000 in civil penalties against three carriers for their roles in causing a lengthy tarmac delay after a flight was diverted to Rochester International Airport in Minnesota due to bad weather.

For the year ending June 30, 2010, the Department issued a total of 37 cease and desist orders against airlines and agents relating to non-safety related aviation matters. Those orders assessed close to $3.2 million in civil penalties. Those numbers reflect a reversal from a downward trend in the prior few years.

Before closing, I would like to thank this Committee and Congress as a whole for helping invigorate our consumer protection program. In the past few years Congress has appropriated additional funds that have enabled us to increase our consumer protection staffing, conduct on-site investigations, and take a number of other proactive steps to support our consumer rulemakings and to strengthen our consumer protection program overall. We also appreciate the work of this Committee's staff, as well as Senate Commerce Committee staff ,who have approached us for technical assistance on the Passenger Rights Legislationcurrently being considered by Congress. We hope these contributions have been helpful to the Committees.

In conclusion Mr. Chairman, we believe we have a high level of appreciation for the many problems faced by airline passengers and we will continue to take aggressive and timely action to mitigate those problems in the future. I want to assure you on behalf of Secretary LaHood and the other employees of the Department of our continuing commitment to this important work. Thank you again for the opportunity to discuss these critical matters. I would be happy to answer any questions you may have.

In: Commercial Airlines: Passenger Fee Issues ISBN: 978-1-61761-989-2
Editors: Michael J. Liguori

Chapter 4

TESTIMONY OF BEN BALDANZA, PRESIDENT AND CEO, SPIRIT AIRLINES, INC., BEFORE THE SUBCOMMITTEE ON AVIATION, HEARING ON "AIRLINE FEES"

Thank you for the opportunity to appear today before the Subcommittee in connection with its review of airline fees. Spirit is based in Fort Lauderdale, Florida. We currently have a fleet of 31 aircraft, serving 44 cities in the U.S., the Caribbean, Central and South America. We carry approximately 6.5 million passengers a year. Spirit believes that "unbundling" - *i.e.*, separating out optional customer services from the fare that are not essential to transporting a passenger allows customers the choice to purchase services or not - benefits the traveling public through lower total costs. This approach generates increased tax revenue by stimulating more travel. These unbundled services do not impose any costs on airport infrastructure, on the nation's air traffic control system or any other government services funded by the aviation federal excise tax. As such, no additional tax burden should be imposed on the cost of these ancillary services.

Over the past decade, the U.S. airline industry has lost approximately $60 billion. In light of the continuing weak economy and reduced demand for air transportation as well as volatile and uncertain fuel prices, imposing additional taxes on the industry and its passengers, will be counterproductive and result in less, rather than more tax revenue. Air transportation is critical to the health and growth of the Country's small and medium sized businesses – indeed its impact is geometric. Raising the cost of travel for these businesses hurts their ability to hire employees and expand.

The best way to enhance tax revenue is to generate more passengers as the country weathers difficult economic times. And the best way to grow traffic is by keeping the total cost of flying as low as possible for the vast majority of travelers.

In 1978 Congress passed the Airline Deregulation Act. The Statement of Policy in the Act specifically found as in the public interest:

encouraging, developing, and maintaining an air transportation system relying on actual and potential competition-

A. *to provide efficiency, innovation, and low prices; and*
B. *to decide on the variety and quality of, and determine prices for, air transportation services.*

Spirit Airlines takes this policy to heart. Our goal is to offer consumers a *real* choice in selecting an airline for their travel needs. Since 2007 when we adopted our Ultra Low Cost Carrier (Ultra LCC) business model, our goal has been to provide basic quality air transportation at the lowest possible price. Spirit's business model to provide maximum choice to passengers to purchase the specific services they want, while keeping fares as low as possible - is unique among U.S. airlines. (See Attachment 1). In many markets Spirit is the only low fare operator and even where other so-called "low cost" carriers operate, Spirit provides an important public interest service by disciplining fares. Spirit's impact was clearly demonstrated when its pilots went on strike last month and other carriers, including low fare carriers, immediately raised prices. For example, JetBlue raised its roundtrip fare in the Fort Lauderdale-San Juan, Puerto Rico market from under $200 to over $600, while at the same time putting out a press release that it was "helping Spirit's customers." Spirit would never seek to take advantage of customers this way. Our approach is to offer the lowest fare all the time on all the routes we fly. While Spirit offers the lowest possible fares, thereby disciplining prices in the 300 plus markets it serves, it operates the most modern fleet of aircraft in the U.S. Over the next five years we will add 35 new aircraft to meet the growing demand for our unique Ultra LCC service.

In an effort to make air fares as low as possible, in 2007 Spirit unbundled the charge for checked bags and, despite rising fuel costs, lowered our base fares to adjust for the unbundling. The per-bag price was set by taking into account our variable and fixed costs associated with processing checked bags. Some other carriers later added similar fees, but only in reaction to higher fuel prices and not with the corresponding drop in the base fare.

This April we announced our decision to charge for carry-on luggage that is too big to fit under the seat, beginning August 1, 2010. This charge does not apply to such items as required medical equipment, baby strollers, etc. The primary reason for the carry-on charge was to reduce the amount of baggage brought into the cabin. Carry-on bags have become a nightmare for passenger boarding and deplaning. They create a safety risk for both passengers and flight attendants and lead to costly flight delays. Significantly, last March the Association of Flight Attendants reported that 80 percent of flight attendants had been injured during the last year by moving carry-on bags in and out of overhead bins.

Carrying more than one bag is not necessary for all travelers and we believe it is unfair to charge those customers for extra services they do not use – indeed, it is the basis for Spirit's policy to unbundle services not essential to passenger transport. The carry on fee for most passengers is $20 - $30. Spirit reduced its base fares to offset these charges. Spirit also lowered its checked bag charge to encourage passengers to check their bags. Passengers can get the lowest price by making these purchases on-line, either when making the booking or prior to check-in. The imposition of the carry-on fee has not affected Spirit bookings, because the total cost to customers for travel on Spirit remains far lower than on other airlines. (See Attachment 2). Overall, bag fees have led to customers packing less and reduced total baggage on flights. This has lowered operating costs and resulted in even fewer lost or damaged bags.

Ancillary Fees Should Not Be Subject to the Federal Excise Tax

As a group, low fare carriers already pay a greater percentage of the total ticket cost in taxes than do the higher fare legacy carriers. This is because much of the tax burden on all airlines is in fixed charges. On a domestic flight, these include, in addition to the 7.5 percent excise tax, the:

- $3.70 segment fee,
- $2.50 September 11th fee
- In many places, a $4.50 per airport PFC, and

- 4.3 cents per gallon commercial jet fuel tax

So for example, on a 300 mile trip with a $180 roundtrip fare, the customer could pay a total of $35.40 in taxes, or approximately 20 percent of the fare including the federal excise tax. Since Spirit has the lowest fares in the industry (See Attachment 2), its lower income passengers are already effectively paying the highest taxes as a percentage of the total fare. This is the unfortunate and regressive result of the current tax structure. We emphasize in this connection that fuel, which has constituted from 35 percent to well over 40 percent of Spirit's total operating costs, is already taxed, which given current fuel prices, is equal to approximately two percent of Spirit fuel costs. Since the cost of fuel is included in the base air fare, there is already clearly some double taxation of air fares. Our average fare is under $85, and our passengers pay over $11 in Federal Excise tax, or 13%, on this amount for just the ticket tax and the fuel tax. Imposing an excise tax on certain ancillary charges, such as for baggage and seat selection will theoretically raise some revenue for the government. However, the primary impact of such a change will be to raise prices for all consumers and thereby dampen travel demand and likely result is less total government excise tax revenue. At a time when the industry has serious financial issues and the Secretary of Transportation has set up a Commission to determine how to strengthen the industry for the benefit of employees, consumers and shareholders, it would be counterproductive to impose yet another tax burden. And we emphasize that given the ultra low fares Spirit offers – fares that enable many to fly for the first time – any additional tax burden will disproportionately hurt the lowest income consumers – the very Americans most hurt by the depressed economy.

As noted, the services Spirit has unbundled do not involve activities that drive up the cost of air traffic control (ATC) services or other services paid for through the aviation trust fund. They are not charges for the "transportation of any person." The handling of checked baggage imposes high labor costs on the airline, but does not touch the ATC system. Allowing passengers to buy specific seats in advance if they choose to do so, is a convenience to passengers, which imposes no system cost. Similarly, the carry on bag charge was imposed to enhance safety and make the travel experience more efficient and enjoyable for our customers. Indeed by reducing delays, it will lessen the pressure on the air traffic control system. The decision to add this fee had nothing to do with avoiding taxes.

Another non-transportation ancillary fee - that imposed for flight changes involving non-refundable tickets - is intended to cover the costs imposed on the airline by such a change. These costs include the direct cost for the time of the reservation agents who process the change. They also contribute to covering other possible lost revenue.

For example a flight change may result in the original flight going out with empty seats – seats which otherwise would have been occupied. Passengers who want to avoid such fees can purchase a higher priced refundable ticket or purchase low-price travel insurance.

Recent articles in the press indicate that based on a 1st Quarter DOT report, Spirit has the highest ancillary revenue as a percent of total revenue. This comparison is highly misleading. Spirit's percentage of ancillary revenue to total revenue is higher than for other carriers simply because our fares are the lowest. For example, if Spirit had the same average fare as American Airlines, its ancillary fees would be only 14.2 percent of total revenue. If its fares were the same as United, Spirit's ancillary fees would be 11.8 percent. Like Continental – 12.3 percent and like Delta – 15 percent.

Over 70 percent of Spirit revenue comes from ticket sales and is subject to the aviation excise tax. Of the 25 percent of revenue that could be labeled ancillary, approximately 60 percent is itinerary related. Within this itinerary related amount, about 50 percent is from baggage fees and 10 percent from seat selection fees. The remaining 40 percent of ancillary revenue comes from subscriptions to our $9 Fare Club, credit card fees, commissions on hotel, car rentals and flight insurance, change fees, on-board food, unaccompanied minor charges, and pet transport. *In total only about 15 percent of Spirit total revenue is from ancillary fees selected by passengers in connection with their travel.*

We are certain that Spirit's decision to unbundle services not essential to the transportation of passengers, has enabled more passengers to fly at lower cost. Indeed given our low fares, it has allowed many to travel who otherwise simply could not afford to do so. Spirit believes these changes have had minimal, if any, negative impact on the total excise taxes paid for travel on Spirit. This is because our lower fares have enabled more people to fly, despite the difficult economy of the last several years. Imposing the excise tax on these fees will simply raise fares, dampen the public's ability to afford travel, and thereby result in lower overall tax revenue.

THERE SHOULD BE GREATER TRANSPARENCY ON FARES

Spirit firmly believes it is in the interest of consumers to be able to access as much information as is reasonably available on the cost of their air travel. Spirit's website provides information on all its charges. Indeed, when booking on Spirit's website, a customer can see the total cost for their flight including all the optional services they have selected before they confirm the purchase. This makes it easy for customers to comparison shop to confirm that Spirit's total price is the lowest.

Unfortunately, under Department of Transportation policy, airlines must include the federal excise tax as part of the base fare whenever a specific fare is listed. Accordingly, under this rule the excise tax component is hidden in the base fare. We are not aware of any other retail product where, by government fiat, merchants are prevented from showing consumers how much of their payment is for tax.

In closing, it is important to point out several particularly onerous proposals recently made by the Department of Transportation. First, although for years the Department has permitted airlines to list certain government taxes and fees - such as the segment fee and the September 11 fee - separately from the base fare when a specific fare is first displayed, it now proposes to require airlines to include all applicable taxes and fees in any initial fare quote. Such an approach will only further obfuscate what is being charged by the airline as opposed to what is going to the government and to airports. We believe Congress should direct the Department to permit airlines to display fares on their websites in a totally transparent way, and specifically in a way that consumers can immediately see how much of their fare goes to pay taxes and other governmental fees.

Second, the Department has asked for comments on requiring carriers to actually show two fares when advertising air fares. One fare would be the carrier's real fare, including all mandatory charges. The other fictional fare would include the "cost of baggage charges that traditionally have been included in the price of the ticket." Such a requirement would not only be costly to implement but would serve no purpose other than to confuse customers who neither need nor want to buy traditional high priced bundled service.

Third, the Department is proposing that all airlines be required to allow customers to hold a booking without payment, or allow a booking to be cancelled without charge for at least 24 hours, even for non-refundable tickets. Many of our promotions are one day sales. Allowing a 24 hour hold would circumvent the sale, resulting in a churn which adds cost and lowers revenue. This will lead to higher fares, again disproportionately penalizing the lowest income American consumers. Holding a product for 24 hours inside a week would be like telling a grocery store they must sell you milk, allow you to hold it for a day and then bring it back, allowing the customer to take away valuable selling time. Most low fare carriers, including Southwest, do not permit either of these options for non-refundable tickets. Such a rule would require substantial and costly changes in our IT reservations system as well as changing the contract with our credit card processing agent. As noted, on Spirit passengers can shop and compare prices before they buy. The proposed rule would not benefit the vast majority of travelers and would simply raise costs. At this painful time of economic malaise, it is essential that government "do no harm" by imposing excessive regulatory requirements.

CONCLUSION

Spirit believes in considering ancillary fees and other consumer "protections," Congress must be guided by the objectives established by the Airline Deregulation Act – namely the encouragement of innovation, competition and the expansion of low fare service. It is of course important for the government to generate sufficient tax revenue to fund that portion of our National airway system that is used by commercial airlines. However, these revenues should be generated by promoting economic expansion and taking steps to encourage more people to fly. Imposing new taxes on fees for customer services that are not essential to the transportation of passengers and are unrelated to costs imposed on the system, must be avoided. Such taxes would surely harm competition, raise costs and slow the industry's recovery from a decade of losses. Most consumers today are very sophisticated about air travel. They have multiple websites from which to obtain fare information. They do not need to see hypothetical, make-believe fares, but rather should be permitted to see what applicable ancillary fees are and how much of their fare goes to the federal excise tax, as well as other government charges. Rules that simply result in higher fares but provide no substantive benefit to customers are not in the public interest and hinder the kind of innovation airline deregulation was intended to promote.

Thank you for your consideration.

Attachment 1

Spirit Is Committed to Delivering Consistent Profitability by Competing on Price

Attachment 2

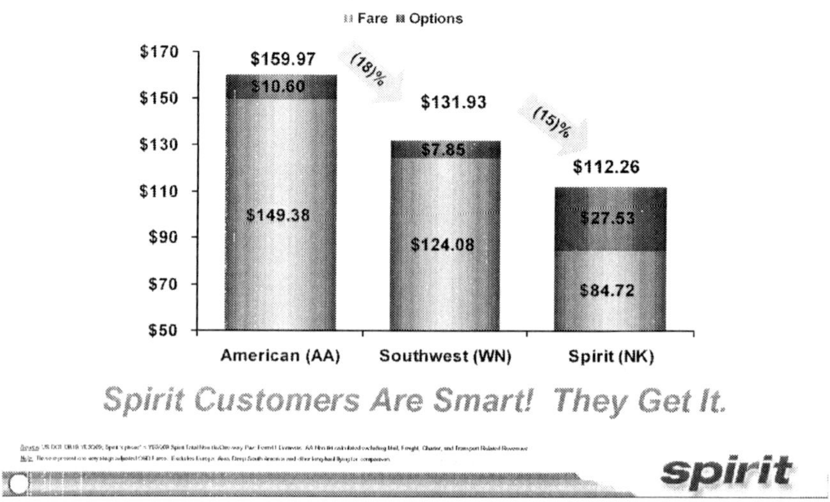

It's The Total Price That Counts

In: Commercial Airlines: Passenger Fee Issues ISBN: 978-1-61761-989-2
Editors: Michael J. Liguori

Chapter 5

TESTIMONY OF DAVE RIDLEY, SENIOR VICE PRESIDENT, MARKETING AND REVENUE MANAGEMENT, SOUTHWEST AIRLINES CO., BEFORE THE SUBCOMMITTEE ON AVIATION, HEARING ON "AIRLINE FEES"

Chairman Costello, Ranking Member Petri and Members of the Subcommittee:

Thank you for inviting Southwest Airlines to testify at today's hearing. My name is Dave Ridley. I'm Senior Vice President of Marketing and Revenue Management for Southwest Airlines and a Southwest Employee since 1988. In my role, I am accountable for the Company's topline revenue performance. My responsibilities include, among other things, pricing, advertising, and maintenance of our brand image as America's leading low fare, high Customer Service airline.

Southwest has been in the airline business for the past 39 years. We began operating in 1971 with three planes and one simple notion: If you deliver your Customers to their destinations when they want to get there, on-time, at a low fare – with friendly policies and even friendlier Employees – people will fly your airline.

And you know what?

It works.

Today, Southwest is the nation's largest airline in terms of domestic passengers, carrying more Customers than any other U.S. airline. We now carry over 100 million passengers a year, serving 69 cities in 35 states. We are also the nation's most heavily unionized airline. And we are the ONLY airline that has not had an involuntary furlough of an Employee since our inception in 1971.

No "Nickel and Diming"

After 39 successful years, we continue to look for ways to differentiate ourselves from other airlines beyond our consistently low fares and great Customer Service. Most recently, we chose to make our affordable, transparent and easy-to-understand pricing structure a focal point in winning the hearts of the flying public by not following the industry trend toward "nickel and diming" our Customers. Our overriding philosophy is to ***not*** charge Customers for things they have historically received for free. That is why Southwest is committed to low fares with no hidden fees – what you see is what you pay.

When you book a ticket on Southwest, you will ***not*** pay a fee to check your first or second bag, or to carry on a bag for that matter. You will ***not*** pay a fee to check your bags curbside. You will ***not*** pay up to $150 to change your reservation. You will ***not*** pay a fee to sit in a window or aisle or exit row seat. You will ***not*** pay a fee to make your reservation over the phone. And you will ***not*** pay a fuel or "peak travel" surcharge fee either.

And, as always, snacks, sodas, smiles and the occasional bad joke are all complimentary at Southwest Airlines.

Refusing to Follow the Pack

The recent proliferation of airline fees can be traced to the Energy Crisis of 2008, when fuel prices spiked to levels never seen before. The fee epidemic worsened during last year's recession when passenger and cargo revenue declined significantly. To generate additional revenue, airlines began assessing new fees for various items and services, many of which had been provided to passengers for free prior to 2008.

Even when Wall Street analysts began calling out Southwest for "leaving money on the table," we declined to join other airlines in charging for first and second checked bags, or for other traditionally customary products and services, because it ran counter to Southwest's principles, which I described above.

Instead, we decided to make our "no nickel and diming" philosophy the focus of our national advertising and leverage the issue which Customers viewed as the most egregious example of unwarranted fees – checked bag fees.

In the fall of 2009 – during football season – we launched a direct assault on bag fees, recruiting our own Employees to play themselves in the spots. We doubled-up our campaign this past winter and we continue to reinforce our commitment not to charge for checked bags, including new signage on the bellies of our aircraft: "Free Bags Fly Here."

In addition, our decision not to charge a fee for checking up to two bags has created an added benefit – more overhead space. At Southwest, we generally have more available overhead space than other airlines, which have "incentivized" their customers to carry their bags onboard rather than pay bag fees.

Due in large part to our "Bags Fly Free" campaign, Southwest has experienced a domestic market share shift worth close to a billion dollars since the introduction of this campaign. As a result, our Customers, Employees and Shareholders have been the beneficiaries of this decision.

Again, Southwest looks for ways to enhance the Customer experience without charging Customers for things they have historically received for free. However, Southwest does charge for optional, enhanced services that are not utilized by a majority of our Customers.

For instance, until last year, Southwest did not allow Customers to bring pets into the cabin (other than those Customers with disabilities who rely on assistance animals). Now, all of our Customers may choose to travel with a small pet for a relatively small fee – $75.

Our Customers now also may choose to have their boarding position reserved automatically - 24 hours prior to departure - rather than reserving it themselves.

Southwest provides this service for a fee of $10 one way. Like pet travel, this is an entirely new service for Southwest's Customers, one not historically offered, and the Customer feedback has been extremely positive.

To Fee or Not to Fee

Our position on fees creates a fortunate alignment of a corporate goal to generate positive financial results with the passion of our People to provide good Customer Service. We listen to our People. (They, in turn, do not shy away from telling us exactly what they think!) Our People told us that THEY don't want us to nickel and dime THEIR Customers. Allowing them to do what they do best, in a Customer friendly way, is just one reason why, since 1987, when the Department of Transportation began tracking Customer Satisfaction statistics, Southwest has consistently led the entire airline industry with the lowest ratio of complaints per passengers boarded. This is further evidence that our policy is not a gimmick – it's good business and it makes our People feel better about who they are and what they do.

While we're not fans of fees for services that historically have been part of the base fare, we believe strongly that the decision on whether or not to charge a fee for an airline product or service is a business decision best made by each individual airline.

Southwest made the conscious decision to limit our Customers' fee exposure to what we view as unreasonable and annoying fees. That was our choice. Other airlines have chosen a different business model and should have every right to do so.

Disclosing Fees is Good Customer Service

Instead, Southwest believes the federal government should focus on ensuring the full and proper disclosure of any and all fees to consumers; making sure that airfares are advertised fairly and honestly. In Southwest Airline's opinion, increasing consumer protections through robust disclosure requirements provides the best Customer Service.

For this reason, Southwest generally supports the Department of Transportation's recent Notice of Proposed Rulemaking with respect to fee disclosure, so that air travelers have accurate and adequate information to make informed decisions when selecting flights. Only an informed consumer can make apples-to-apples fare comparisons, which allows them to shop for a flight that best meets their needs and preferences.

As the number and complexity of ancillary fees increase, we believe additional disclosure is necessary to ensure air travelers have access to information on charges that may be added to their base fare. To protect the traveling public, fees should be prominently disclosed to consumers wherever tickets are sold. We believe the DOT's NPRM would achieve this goal.

On behalf of Southwest Airlines, thank you for this opportunity to testify. I will be happy to answer any questions.

In: Commercial Airlines: Passenger Fee Issues ISBN: 978-1-61761-989-2
Editors: Michael J. Liguori

Chapter 6

TESTIMONY OF KEVIN P. MITCHELL, CHAIRMAN, BUSINESS TRAVEL COALITION, BEFORE THE SUBCOMMITTEE ON AVIATION, HEARING ON "AIRLINE FEES"

Mr. Chairman, Ranking Member Petri, and Members of the Subcommittee thank you for requesting that Business Travel Coalition (BTC) appear before you today to represent consumer and corporate managed travel interests on the subjects of airline product unbundling and extra fees for consumers.

My testimony today marks the 21st time BTC has been asked to provide testimony in Congress on competition, security and passenger rights issues. Today's hearing is by far the most important in terms of an issue's potential for harmful impacts to competition and consumers. BTC is not against unbundling as a matter of principle, but rather, it is opposed to the absence of disclosure of all fees and charges such that consumers cannot fully benefit from comparative shopping.

I. INDUSTRY CONTEXT

By way of industry context, airline product unbundling and ancillary fees took off like a rocket in the U.S. during the past 24 months such that the whole industry was caught off guard without systems and processes to properly identify, manage and control these expenses. In particular, corporate travel managers are on the receiving end of this industry surprise.

Thus far, multiple airlines dissecting the airline product in differing ways and then levying new and varying fees for services long included as part of the ticket price has caused significant new complexities and costs as well as obstacles for effectively managing corporate travel programs. Never has there been an opportunity for such serious bedlam in managed travel. Helter Skelter has become the rule of the day in airline pricing. Indeed, it's hard to find a corporate travel manager who supports this new industry direction, as currently implemented.

BTC yesterday published the survey results of 188 business travel industry professionals concerning airline fees and unbundling. The top-line results underscore deep concerns and the need for government oversight.

Consider:

- 100% of corporate travel managers indicated that unbundling and these extra fees have caused serious problems for their managed travel programs.
- 86% of travel managers believe that airlines, *absent government regulation*, will not make fair, adequate and readily accessible disclosure of their extra fees and charges so that travel managers and/or their TMCs can do comparison shopping of the all-in prices for air travel across carriers.
- 95% of travel managers support the proposal that the U.S. DOT require airlines to make ancillary fee data available and easily accessible to the travel agency channel through any GDS in which that airline has agreed to participate.
- 95% of travel managers do not support an airline distribution model wherein access to airfare and ancillary servicescontent is available only on airlines' websites, or through direct connections to multiple airlines' inventory systems.

I should hasten to point out that survey participants are business people who, as a general proposition, do not favor government intervention in a marketplace. However, as with BTC, who testified four times since 1999 against passenger rights legislation, these industry experts lived through 10 years of airline stonewalling and broken promises and finally realized that the airlines were never going to take extended tarmac delays seriously until made to do so. Travel managers and travel agency executives do not want to wait 10 years, or even 1 more year to see if the airlines will properly disclose their ancillary fees in all channels in which they sell their products - and thus already make their published, but now incomplete, fares available.

In addition to managed travel issues, there are significant consumer issues.

In the leisure and unmanaged travel segments, the unbundling concept could succeed or fail based upon millions of individual purchasing decisions as well as competitive responses. Some consumers will value the different choices; others will feel they are being "nickel and dimed." Still others could become confused should all carriers eventually unbundle without uniform standards, adding great complexity at the industry level. As Procter & Gamble acknowledged in the 1990s, 27 varieties, *of just its shampoo*, on a supermarket shelf does not necessarily equate to consumer choice, but often consumer confusion.

What's more, with such across-the-board unbundling of the price to be paid for the travel services desired, consumers may not have any ability to evaluate the full price of the several air travel options available. Today, these unbundled elements of the price to be paid for air travel are missing entirely in the responses of travel agencies to fare shopping entries that seek to compare prices across carriers. Nearly all travel agencies, and thus nearly all corporate travel departments, depend on GDSs for all their fare information. Accordingly, this current opaque approach by airlines to pricing will inevitably impede a consumer's search for low fares. As one does not usually see these "extras" until well into the transaction, a large segment of consumers will not start over in the quest for low fares by looking at alternative airlines. Economists will say that anything that increases "consumer search costs" invariably raises prices paid.

Consumer and passenger advocates could argue persuasively that unbundling, which results in airline products looking less expensive in GDSs and website shopping inquiries than would likely be the case after the extras are piled on, results in higher prices paid because with search costs increased, more shoppers will just miss a de facto lower "all-in" fare that includes the extras. The game could be viewed as bait-and-switch: from an ostensibly lower fare to an actual higher fare.

The Consumer Travel Alliance just published an analysis that vividly shows how unsuspecting consumers can become entrapped by hidden fees upon arrival at the airport. The analysis focused on four popular flight itineraries taken by millions of travelers each year - New York-Los Angeles, Boston-Washington, Chicago-Miami, and Washington-Orlando – and included just two of the common fees now charged by airlines: checked baggage and extra legroom.

Consider:

- A typical traveler requesting extra legroom and checking a single bag would pay an average of one-quarter (26%) more than the base price of the ticket shown on the website.
- A traveler checking two bags would pay more than half the price of the ticket in additional fees that were hidden at the time of the transaction (54%).
- The amount of hidden fees charged to a typical traveler with a single bag ranged from 10% to 82% of the price of the base fare.
- The amount of hidden fees charged to a typical traveler with two bags ranged from 21% to 153% of the price of the base fare.

II. Why Are Some Airlines Apparently Stonewalling Again?

a. To be painfully honest, major network airlines often have a strong incentive to mislead consumers. They remain at a 30% to 35% cost disadvantage against low-cost carriers (LCCs), and as such, cannot offer the kind of across-the-board low fares the LCCs do. There is a motivation present to obfuscate the true all-in price by hiding fees and especially resisting efforts to have fees and fares made available in a comparative display for travel agents via the global distribution systems (GDSs).

b. The Airline Tariff Publishing Company (ATPCO) has a data system tested by 27 airlines - including all the major U.S. airlines - and ready to go to facilitate the loading of ancillary fees in the GDSs and their comparative presentation on travel agents' screens. However, not a single major U.S. has signed on to use the new system because the first airline to do so will likely show higher all-in fares by 30% or more than competitors. In an industry where a few dollars can make the difference for a consumer in choosing one airline over another, this could be the equivalent of competitive suicide.

c. Some airlines would like to force GDSs and travel agencies to pay for access to their unbundled services; an audacious play to shift the costs of merchandising and distributing their products and services onto the backs of consumers who are already paying for these business activities in the prices of their tickets.

III. FALSE ARGUMENTS

a. Some airlines may argue that the cost of making ancillary fees widely available to consumers would be too high. However, participation in ATPCO's new system would cost just $3,000 per month, per airline. Surely, this is a false argument given the billions of dollars being collected for ancillary fees.

b. Other airlines may argue that there are technical impediments to providing such data to consumers, but 27 airlines have successfully tested ATPCO's new system. So one would naturally ask why as to the disclosure of fees airlines cannot do what the airline-owned ATPCO says 27 of them are doing and that ATPCO says six pricing systems, including the three GDSs, are receiving and testing?

c. Airlines can be expected to complain that the U.S. DOT's Notice of Proposed Rulemaking (NPRM) is "interference in the marketplace." However, the airlines have the data now; the technology solution has been developed by ATPCO; and the $36,000 per year cost is insignificant. How can airlines then oppose DOT's anticipated rule to require them to provide the fee data in an easily usable and accessible manner for travel agencies via the GDSs in which they participate? DOT is not endeavoring to regulate the marketplace, but to ensure adequate disclosure practices.

d. Airlines claim they have no obligation to provide fee data to travel agencies. However, agents are the legal agents of the airlines, and as such, how can airlines not provide all pricing information to them? If an airline has decided to agree with a GDS that agents using that system can sell the airline's fares, then partial disclosure of the entire price for the services the travelers need or want by not providing the data on extra charges in an electronic and easily accessible way via that GDS is just not a defensible option. It is deceptive per se. Airlines are in effect trying to make only a part of the airfare visible; they are not providing the entire fare.

IV. Consumer Protection's No Man's Land!

a. The federal government should be impelled to provide detailed and meaningful consumer protections in commercial air transportation because unlike the case in nearly all other industries consumers have no protections against unfair or deceptive practices by airlines from the FTC and no legal rights under state laws to seek redress for abysmal treatment because of federal preemption -- a doctrine the airlines have championed and fight hammer-and-tong to defend and expand. Moreover, under federal law (49 USC Section 41712) consumers do not have a right to sue for bad service. In the currently open NPRM, DOT recognizes the uniquely vulnerable position of air travelers in this virtual no man's land. In short, except to the extent Congress or DOT mandates specific consumer protections, consumers are

b. It is highly significant that the DOT economic analysis underpinning its NPRM found that while all four of the online travel agencies (OTAs) displayed the "entire price" of a ticket including government and airport charges for different travel options (data currently available in the GDSs), only one of eight airline websites did. This marked difference in approach to disclosure can perhaps be explained by the fact that OTAs and brick-and-mortar travel agencies have no inherent economic incentive to collect higher as opposed to lower prices for airline tickets. Most importantly, this finding by DOT underscores the needed, pro-consumer role that travel agencies and OTAs can play in spurring airlines themselves to make better disclosure of the entire price including ancillary fees on their websites. Of course, travel agencies and OTAs cannot carry out this salutary mission unless carriers are required to provide them via the GDSs on which they rely for fare information the airlines' data specifying their extra fees and charges.

V. Congress Can Make A Difference

The single most important step this Committee can take is to urge the DOT, through its NPRM, that in addition to requiring airlines to make add-on fee data available and easily accessible on their websites that they should be required to make that same fee data available to the travel agency channel through any GDS in which that airline has agreed to participate. Congress could also provide this relief in the FAA Reauthorization Act through Senator Menendez's sensible disclosure proposal.

In: Commercial Airlines: Passenger Fee Issues ISBN: 978-1-61761-989-2
Editors: Michael J. Liguori

Chapter 7

STATEMENT OF KYLE MOORE, VICE-PRESIDENT, MARKETING, SABRE HOLDINGS, ON BEHALF OF THE INTERACTIVE TRAVEL SERVICES ASSOCIATION, AMERICAN SOCIETY OF TRAVEL AGENTS, AND CONSUMER TRAVEL ALLIANCE, BEFORE THE SUBCOMMITTEE ON AVIATION, HEARING ON "AIRLINE FEES"

Good afternoon, Mr. Chairman, Ranking Member Petri, and Members of the Subcommittee. The Interactive Travel Services Association (ITSA), American Society of Travel Agents (ASTA) and the Consumer Travel Alliance (CTA) all appreciate the opportunity to present our views on airline add-on fees and charges, and making them as transparent to consumers as possible.

My name is Kyle Moore, and I am the Vice President for Marketing of Sabre Holdings, owner of both the Sabre Network Global Distribution System (GDS), and Travelocity, an online travel company (OTC). Both are leaders in their fields, with our GDS, the largest in the United States, serving as the intermediary between airlines and other travel providers and thousands of travel agencies, including both traditional "brick-and-mortar" agencies and OTCs. All of those travel agency users rely on the computer reservations system provided by the Sabre GDS for timely, accurate and comprehensive air travel pricing and availability information on our nearly 400 participating airlines. Sabre is a long-time and active member of both ITSA and ASTA.

ITSA is the trade association for OTCs and GDSs, and is their voice on matters of public policy. ITSA seeks to promote consumer choice, access, confidence, protection and information in the world of online travel, and to develop consensus among industry, consumer organizations and policy makers on issues related to consumer use of the Internet to meet their needs.

ASTA is the largest association of professional travel retailers in the world. Its mission is to facilitate the business of selling travel through effective representation, shared knowledge and the enhancement of professionalism. ASTA seeks a retail travel marketplace that is profitable and growing and a rewarding field in which to work, invest and do business. See www.asta.org.

CTA is a non-profit organization created to inform and educate legislators, regulators and their staffs about policy issues affecting the travel needs of consumers. The alliance is a member of the Consumer Federation of America. CTA is intimately involved with the current conference committee negotiation over the Federal Aviation Administration Reauthorization. The alliance is also working with state regulators, the Federal Trade Commission and the Department of Transportation on privacy issues, travel insurance, and other pressing consumer issues with online and traditional travel agents and in the area of travelers' rights.

ITSA, ASTA and CTA do not object to airlines' "unbundling" and charging separately for services that have traditionally been included in the prices paid for airline tickets. However, these organizations believe that, regrettably, the proliferation of add-on fees and charges has created such a broad array of potential fees for consumers that the risk of confusion and unpleasant surprises at the airport -- absent full and timely disclosure -- is unacceptably high.

At least 50% of consumers purchasing an airline ticket do so through intermediaries such as OTCs and traditional travel agents because they prefer shopping at comprehensive outlets that offer the flights and fares of numerous airlines. As a matter of first principles, ITSA, ASTA and CTA are convinced that this enormous segment of the traveling public is no less deserving of consumer protection than those travelers who prefer to buy tickets directly from the airlines.

TRANSPARENCY IS THE SOLUTION: ALL ADD-ON FEES SHOULD BE FULLY DISCLOSED PRIOR TO PURCHASE

We believe that the solution is transparency -- full disclosure of information about airline add-on services and fees to consumers when they need it: when those consumers are comparing prices for the full cost of travel prior to purchase.[1] Transparency will safeguard the overriding interest of air travelers in not being confused or, worse, misled, about the price to be paid for air travel and yet not inhibit airlines from unbundling services if they choose.

All airlines should provide full information about all of their add-on fees and charges directly to those consumers who buy tickets from the airlines themselves and, just as importantly, to the GDSs in which they have agreed to participate so that the information can be made available to travel agencies and OTCs for adequate and timely disclosure and sale to consumers. Unfortunately, we are quite concerned that airlines have not, and will not, share information on their add-on services and fees to GDSs and agencies.

While we certainly understand the need for airlines to increase their revenues through add-on fees to shore up their financial condition, broad disclosure of such fees can and does have a positive effect on competition. This benefits consumers both through moderating prices and product innovation. Further, disclosure to agencies allows comparison shopping on a single OTC site or through an interface with a travel agency. This comparison shopping, a major advantage of agency distribution, benefits consumers and contributes to enhanced airline competition generally. This holds true not only for airline fares, but would undoubtedly just as well for add-on fees should information on those fees be provided by the airlines.

ITSA, ASTA and CTA support legislation to reauthorize the Federal Aviation Administration. More specifically to the issues raised at this hearing, we support provisions in that legislation that would ensure transparency and full disclosure of information to consumers at the time of shopping and purchase. This notably includes the amendment added to the Senate bill by Senators Menendez and Schumer that would require it. We urge full support of that amendment in conference, including a key adjustment endorsed by both these Senators and other Members that would require the information be shared in a timely way through all intermediaries, such as GDSs, in which an airline participates.

Moreover, the Department of Transportation is currently conducting a rulemaking to generally enhance passenger protections under its legal authority to protect consumers from unfair or deceptive practices.[2] Current airfare regulations under this authority were written when fees for all air carriage services were included in the overall ticket price. As those services and fees are being unbundled, DoT is appropriately updating its regulations to ensure consumers will still be adequately protected. Among the changes DoT is considering is requiring the airlines to fully and timely furnish information about their add-on fees and charges to intermediaries through the GDSs in which the airlines make their basic fares available. ITSA, *ASTAand CTA* will be filing comments urging adoption of this requirement.

In my testimony today, in addition to discussing transparency, I will provide an overview of the relationships between airlines and their third-party intermediaries through the distributive services of the GDSs. That overview will include how content on airfares, schedules, code shares and more is provided, and updated some five times a day, to the GDSs through a clearinghouse created by the airlines: the Airline Tariff Publishing Company (ATPCO). It will also include a brief review of the multi-industry party effort to create the technical standards to similarly provide and update information on ancillary fares through a new protocol called ATPCO OC. That protocol has been tested by more than 20 airlines, including most of the US major carriers, and is ready for implementation.

Background on, and the Accelerating Momentum of, Unbundling

For decades, the "all-in price" of the basic elements of the air travel experience for nearly all travelers was reflected in the fares that airlines published and that the airlines and travel agents[3] – who are the legal agents of airlines for the sale of tickets – communicated to ultimate consumers before they committed to a travel purchase. As a consequence, the full and inclusive price of each of the travel options on numerous airlines being considered by a consumer was easy to determine. Consumers benefitted enormously from this pricing transparency.

Over the last two to three years, the airline pricing regime has changed radically. Airlines have "unbundled" their product, and many are now levying significant add-on fees and charges for services once widely taken for granted as included in the ticket price. The most notable example of this trend is checked baggage fees. The common, long-standing practice in the airline industry was to allow each passenger to check two bags without extra charge as part of the basic service rendered for the fare paid, subject to certain size and weight restrictions.

Today, by contrast, a passenger traveling domestically on nearly all of the major U.S. airlines who checks two standard size suitcases would be charged somewhere between $55 and $60 each way. Assuming an average round-trip ticket price of $300 for U.S. domestic travel, that extra fee is significant for most consumers – representing a price increase of roughly 40% over the "published" fare. It is beyond debate that in most circumstances an airline charging such a premium on the fare itself would expect notable losses of market share to other airlines with competitive schedules. Moreover, some of the competitors of these large carriers charge lower fees for two items of checked baggage (such as AirTran and JetBlue), or no such fees at all, as is the case with Southwest.

Given the widely reported new policies by U.S. airlines on the size and number of bags that can be carried onboard, with many travelers being compelled to check their luggage, these sizable fees cannot be readily avoided by many consumers. For example, a family of four, consisting of two adults and two young children, booking a week-long vacation could hardly be expected to travel with carry-on baggage alone. Thus, there can be little doubt that the fees an airline imposes for checked baggage should be clearly and effectively communicated to consumers before they are locked into a purchasing decision in order to avoid widespread consumer deception about a matter of the utmost importance – i.e., the price paid for the services to be used.

Therefore, the disclosure provisions added to the FAA Reauthorization bill are quite welcome. Moreover, DoT has maintained a policy since 2008 requiring appropriate disclosure by airlines of their checked baggage charges in advertisements. However, the critical problem that remains in both the proposed legislation (as currently written) and DoT's checked baggage policy is the absence of a requirement that each airline provide the travel agents on whose behalf they sell tickets the needed baggage and other add-on fee information in a usable, reliable and efficient manner. In other words, the information may be available for passengers who deal directly with the airline, but it is not available for the large percentage of passengers that choose to work through online and traditional travel agencies.

To obtain add-on fee information is a time-consuming, manual process that is overwhelming and simply does not work for traditional travel agents or OTCs – all of whom operate in a very competitive business where efficiency is paramount. Today, they must resort to reviewing carriers' websites, and waiting for their news releases or reports in the trade or general media. In order to stay abreast of constantly changing ancillary fees at potentially hundreds of airlines, they would have to substantially add to staff, which is unaffordable. This process is highly ineffective and unworkable, in contrast to the situation with airline fares, which airlines do share with their agencies in a timely, robust manner through the GDSs or otherwise.

The potential for consumer harm is great here. As I noted above, more than one half of all air travel is sold in the United States by travel agencies, as contrasted with the airlines directly.[4] In a nutshell, while airlines have been energetically engaged in various efforts to dissect the air transportation product and assess these new fees, the industry has been slow and apparently reluctant to develop vehicles for effectively and timely communicating to the agencies information on add-on services and fees.

The new and substantial charges for checked luggage were only the vanguard of added fees imposed on consumers for services once included in the published fare. For example, AirTran levies an added roundtrip fee of $40 to reserve an exit row seat, and Frontier assesses a roundtrip fee of $30-$50 for the right to reserve a seat with "extra legroom." Recognizing that both United and US Airways already impose additional charges for premium seat selection in economy, the recent announcement by Continental that it too will impose a new charge for extra legroom increases the chances that unbundled premium seat charges will become a new norm. Moreover, Spirit has added yet another unbundling innovation: charges for carry-on bags.

Further, some airlines impose a fee to purchase any seat on their aircraft in advance of check-in, with higher fees imposed for perceived preferred seats. On these airlines, a passenger therefore now purchases air transportation through the base fare, but must then separately purchase a seat on the plane unless the passenger waits until 24 hours before check-in, at which time a specific seat can either be purchased or one will be assigned without a fee (from, predictably, inferior seat positions remaining at that time). Consider the impracticality of this for that same family of four traveling together.

Among a litany of others, examples of additional services for which carriers have begun charging consumers fees are:

- Blankets/pillows in flight – American charges $8, JetBlue $7, USAir $7, and Virgin America $12, with the rest of the carriers apparently charging nothing at the moment.

- Meals – while most carriers assess some charge on coach passengers for an in-flight meal, at the moment Continental and JetBlue appear to offer meals on some flights with no added fee.
- WIFI – charges vary widely by carrier, with our research suggesting American Airlines charges a fee of $10-$13 and Continental $4.95 but with a price that varies by usage in the case of Continental.

Undoubtedly, there is more unbundling of airline pricing to come. While we are neutral on the decisions of the airlines to unbundle their fares, we do object to unbundling of airline pricing in the absence of the airlines disclosing their add-on fees and charges to their agents in an effective, efficient, usable and timely manner. Without such disclosure by the airlines, travel agencies have no practical, workable way to acquire the information they must have in order to disclose to the traveling public the full, all-in price of each of the options the traveler is considering. As a result, consumers are unable to engage in meaningful comparative shopping among airlines because large elements of the full price for travel are missing from the agency websites and from the data available to travel agents. Competition is enhanced when consumers have more information, not less.

On that score, it is widely known that air travelers are highly price sensitive, with a fare differential of even a few dollars regarded by airlines as sufficient to drive consumers to choose one alternative over another. Since consumer behavior has demonstrated irrefutably that even a few dollars are critical in making an air travel buying decision, any airline pricing regime that fails to ensure travel agencies are equipped with this key information about charges for add-ons generates substantial risk of broad consumer confusion, if not functional deception. Failing to adequately, or at all, disclose a $60 fee each way could mislead consumers into picking a flight they would not otherwise choose when there was an alternative flight with zero baggage fees. The larger the amount assessed the more compelling the need for full and fair disclosure.

In the United States today, nearly all travel agencies continue to heavily rely on GDSs to obtain information on airline fares and to book the airline tickets they sell. They do so because of the enormous efficiency these systems offer, providing in a neutral, unbiased manner easy-to-use data on scores of airlines with just a few keystrokes. By enabling fare transparency, the GDSs have, indeed, been a major force over time for saving consumers hundreds of millions of dollars annually – permitting travel agencies to perform in a few seconds an apples-to-apples comparison of the full price of *all* travel options in a particular market. Nonetheless, GDSs can only provide their travel agency subscribers – brick-and-mortar and OTC – the pricing data that the airlines in turn supply to them.

ATPCO OC: A New Industry Standard in Place to Communicate Add-on Fees

Fortunately, essential industry standards for enabling efficient communication of add-on fees to GDSs have been developed recently. These standards are now provided through an information clearinghouse established by the airlines, the Airline Tariff Publishing Company ("ATPCO"), through a newly-launched product called "ATPCO OC" (also referred to as ATPCO Optional Services and Branded Fares). Importantly, ATPCO OC establishes over 100 unique fields that can be used by airlines to identify, and file their fees and services for, any particular ancillary fee they choose to assess. The GDSs are now completing the system modifications required to display the data to their subscribers in ways that will effect the needed disclosures. More than 20 airlines have tested the system successfully, and the GDSs will begin adding that data to their "live" travel agency displays in coming weeks and months. Attached is an appendix that describes the ATPCO – GDS process in detail, including a roll-out of ATPCO-OC and its capabilities, beginning this month, by using the Sabre system as a proxy for the industry.

Of course, ATPCO OC is very welcome news. However, ATPCO OC can be a fix to the problem of inadequate disclosure by airlines of this vital pricing information to their lawful agents only if all the airlines that engage in unbundling actually utilize ATPCO OC to transmit this data to the GDSs. Unfortunately, to date, while approximately 86% of US point-of-sale bookings are covered by those airlines that have "test-filed" ancillary data via ATPCO, no airlines – to my knowledge – have definitively and publicly indicated that they will continue to provide the necessary information via ATPCO for long term use within the industry.

In fact, we are concerned that airlines have a disincentive to provide the data, as that data would make the prices of their products seem higher. Every airline would of course prefer to appear lower-priced than its competitors for the longest possible time. Thus, powerful economic motivation exists for airlines not to provide the add-on price information to the GDSs.

Therefore, airlines should not be permitted to assess, before or at check-in, add-on fees and charges unless that airline timely makes detailed fee information available to its ticket agents in the same way and at the same time that it makes available to the GDSs information on its fares. Absent a consumer-protection requirement in this area, consumers are destined to be left in the dark.

In other words, through ATPCO OC there is a process and technologies in place right now for full disclosure of add-on fees that will work across all channels which provide information on airfares to consumers. But it will not work at all unless content is supplied by the airlines in a comprehensive and timely way. Without the provision of that content, these advanced and consumer-friendly information solutions will be all dressed up, but have nowhere to go.

Again, Mr. Chairman, ITSA, ASTA and CTA are very pleased to have had this opportunity to communicate our views on the very important matter of fully, usefully and timely disclosing of airline ancillary fare information to the flying public no matter the channel -- directly from airlines or via any intermediary in which an airline participates -- they choose to use.

Thank you, and I will be happy to answer any questions you may have.

End Notes

[1] Concerning when that time would be defined to be, while airlines generally are likely to offer all ancillary services for sale at the time of initial booking, there could be situations where they do not. For example, an airline might decide to offer a fare for sale that expressly does not include various items which it then would later offer for purchase by travelers who bought the fare earlier. In situations such as this, travel agents and OTCs must also have access to the services and fees information at that time, not just at the time of initial booking.

[2] 49 USC 41712

[3] The term "ticket agent" includes both traditional "brick and mortar" agencies and OTCs.

[4] A whitepaper recently authored by PhoCusWright, the air travel industry analytical authority, which underscores the importance of the travel agency network in distributing air transportation, with a specific focus on the role of the GDSs in the distribution chain. A copy of that paper: "The Role and Value of the Global Distribution Systems in Travel Distribution," can be found on the ITSA website: www.interactivetravel.org.

Chapter Sources

The following chapters have been previously published:

Chapter 1 – This is an edited, excerpted and augmented edition of a United States Government Accountability Office publication, Report Order Code GAO-10-785, dated July 2010.

Chapter 2 – This is an edited, excerpted and augmented edition of a United States House of Representatives Committee on Transportation and Infrastructure publication, dated July 12, 2010.

Chapter 3 – These remarks were delivered as Statement of Robert S. Rivkin, before the U.S. House of Representatives Subcommittee on Aviation, given July 14, 2010.

Chapter 4 – These remarks were delivered as Statement of Ben Baldanza, before the U.S. House of Representatives Subcommittee on Aviation, given July 14, 2010.

Chapter 5 – These remarks were delivered as Statement of Dave Ridley before the U.S. House of Representatives Subcommittee on Aviation, given July 14, 2010.

Chapter 6 – These remarks were delivered as Statement of Kevin Mitchell before the U.S. House of Representatives Subcommittee on Aviation, given July 14, 2010.

Chapter 7 – These remarks were delivered as Statement of Kyle Moore before the U.S. House of Representatives Subcommittee on Aviation, given July 14, 2010.

INDEX